HANDBOOKS

Primary Teaching Methods

Dawn Quist

MACMILLAN

First published 2000 by
MACMILLAN EDUCATION LTD
London and Oxford
Companies and representatives throughout the world

ISBN 0-333-72055-5

10 9 8 7 6 5 4 3 2 1
09 08 07 06 05 04 03 02 01 00

This book is printed on paper suitable for recycling and made from fully managed and sustained forest sources.

Printed in Malaysia

A catalogue record for this book is available from the British Library.

Illustrations by Gay Galsworthy

Cover design by Charles Design Associates

Contents

Preface

Improving the quality of teaching at primary school level has been a major concern among education authorities, teacher educators and trainers, teachers' professional organisations, as well as among primary teachers themselves. The need to improve the professional training and performance of teachers is widely accepted. Research and field experience have made us understand better the factors that contribute to developing effective teaching methodologies. We know, for example, that the demands of today's primary education call for teachers who are well skilled and grounded in knowledge, values, and teaching strategies which facilitate creation of an enabling teaching and learning environment.

To provide this teachers need to demonstrate among other factors, knowledge of child development, gender sensitivity, appropriate attitudes to teaching, and skills in organising lessons, lesson planning, working with children, teaching methods, teaching strategies, working with others, assessing pupils' diverse work and activities, and selection of the best resources to support the teaching and learning process. This book deals with all these key elements in the organisation, planning and delivery of effective lessons. Dawn Quist has presented teaching practice activities, techniques and the methods of teaching in simple language. Her effort to bring out the salient features of teaching at primary school level deserves high appreciation.

This book is intended to assist front-line practitioners seeking best practice strategies in teaching at primary school level. As policy-makers on teacher education and training read through the book, it will become clear the author has covered aspects that are truly international. The book will be useful in both developed and developing countries, particularly in countries which have initiated reforms in teacher education and training.

I commend this comprehensive, well-written, readable book to all pre-service and in-service primary teacher educators, co-ordinators and managers of teacher resource centres, primary school heads, serving primary school teachers, student teachers on teaching practice and primary school inspectors.

Dr Henry L. Kaluba
Chief Programme Officer
Education Department
Commonwealth Secretariat
London

Macmillan Teaching Handbooks: Primary Teaching Methods

Introduction

Macmillan Teaching Handbooks

This series has been designed for student and practising primary teachers in African schools. It has been developed as a result of consultation with practising teachers, student teachers and college teacher trainers. The series includes this book, *Primary Teaching Methods*, and one for each of the main subjects: English, Science, Mathematics, and Environmental and Social Studies. All the books cover upper and lower primary.

The books are designed to be used by unqualified or newly qualified teachers, by students studying on formal college courses and by experienced teachers who wish to improve their practice. Readers are encouraged to try out methods and strategies to improve learning and to reflect on their own teaching, either individually or in groups. The material can also be used in Teacher Training College courses or equally effectively in school-based staff development programmes supported by the headteacher, teachers themselves or by primary school advisors.

The books present the material in an attractive, easy to use form, without compromising on concept level, coverage or depth. They make no assumptions about previous study or knowledge, avoid jargon and use clear language. They provide a wealth of practical suggestions and ideas, keeping in mind the problems and challenges that teachers face in the classroom.

Primary Teaching Methods

This book covers all that the aspiring or busy teacher needs to know about the basic methods of primary teaching. It has been written to help teachers develop their professional skills by reflecting on their classroom practice, their approaches to teaching and to the learning of their pupils.

The book has nine sections on basic principles, organisation, planning, working with children, teaching strategies, methods, resources, assessment and working with others. Each section is divided into a number of topics. The sections and topics have been grouped in a particular order to lead readers through the important ideas and issues, but the book does not have to be read through from the beginning. Readers may have different priorities and each topic, while designed to stand on its own, has been linked to others by extensive cross-referencing. This means that readers can quickly and easily refer to particular topics and linked themes.

Each topic covers either one or two double-page spreads, containing background information and activities to encourage readers to try out new ideas. They include information about current theory, simple definitions of common terms or examples of approaches that other teachers have found effective. All topics contain activities to help teachers develop as professionals. These encourage readers to:

- assess their own knowledge and skills;
- become more aware of material and human resources available in the local community and use them in more creative ways;
- develop a variety of teaching methods and strategies that will improve the learning of their pupils.

Primary Teaching Methods

Section 1 Basic principles

1 Knowledge

> *What kind of knowledge do teachers need?*
>
> **Subject knowledge** most primary teachers are required to teach a wide range of subjects.
>
> **Theories of child development** the different stages in the physical, emotional and intellectual development of children.
>
> **Theories of learning** the process of learning, motivation and the use of rewards and punishments to change behaviour.
>
> **Teaching methods** understanding which of the range of methods is the most effective for particular learning situations.
>
> **Classroom management** the process of organising pupils, resources and the learning activities.
>
> **Self knowledge** your own strengths and weaknesses as a teacher.

Subject knowledge

In most countries, the primary curriculum includes at least eight and sometimes as many as fourteen different subjects. Many teachers are aware that they do not know enough about some of these subjects, as they did not study them at school or during their initial teacher training.

This section will look at one area, subject knowledge, that concerns most primary teachers. The other kinds of knowledge are dealt with in later sections.

What are the main problems?

We all have some teaching subjects we like better than others, and some that we do not feel confident about. Almost all teachers admit that they find some subjects or topics more difficult to teach than others. There are three main problems.

- Lack of knowledge of subjects such as Science and Technology, or of particular topics such as magnets or local history.
- Teaching a new topic for the first time.
- How to answer difficult questions such as 'How do birds fly?' or 'Where does the sun go at night?'.

> ## *Activity* Identifying my areas of confidence
>
> Make a list of the subjects that you are expected to teach. Rate each on a scale of 1–3.
>
> **1** = I feel completely confident teaching this subject with my existing knowledge.
>
> **2** = I feel fairly confident but would like some help from colleagues or access to more resource books and material.
>
> **3** = I would be more confident if I had help and further training in this subject.
>
> Then place your teaching subjects in order of your preference, identifying your own areas of competence and those you would like to improve.

How can you overcome these problems?

Subject knowledge is built up over time. Even if you studied a particular subject at school or during your initial teacher training, you will need to up-date your knowledge. You will also have to study new topics that have to be taught in the syllabus.

Make time to study

Make sure that you have read the latest subject manuals issued by your government. If you do not have copies of your own, ask the headteacher or other teachers in the school if you can borrow their manuals for a while. Visit the local Teachers' Resource Centre and see what they have there that will help you. You may find reference books that will give you the facts you need and make you more confident about answering your pupils' questions.

Share knowledge

Learn to share knowledge with your colleagues, the pupils' parents or local experts. In some schools teachers work together and spend an hour each week, after school, planning their approach to particular topics. Even if your school has very few teachers this is still a valuable activity as it allows you to learn from the experience of the head, parents or teachers in other schools.

Practise

After the initial lesson preparation give yourself time to rehearse. Teachers are like actors. Their performance improves and they gain confidence when they have had time to practise what they have to say. This is particularly important if you are going to demonstrate an experiment during your lesson.

Try to think ahead about the questions pupils might ask. There will always be some that you cannot answer. Turn a difficult question into a learning experience. Admit immediately if you do not know the answer. Then involve your pupils in finding the answer for themslves. Ask them to suggest how/where you can all look for the answer. Do any parents know a lot about the subject? A game ranger, for example, will know a lot about animals and the environment.

2 Attitudes to teaching

Activity *Which words would you use to describe your job as a teacher?*

boring; challenging; hard work; time consuming; rewarding; difficult; creative; something to do until I get a better job; interesting; my chosen career; depressing; too little pay for too much work; worthwhile.

Even though conditions are difficult you need to feel positive about your job.

Attitudes to work

Your attitude to teaching and learning and your relationship with your class can have a marked effect on pupil attitudes and learning.

Earning respect

Try to be someone your pupils admire and always set a good example.

- Arrive at the class well prepared and on time.
- Show interest in and enthusiasm for the subjects you teach.
- Look out for interesting objects, articles in newspapers and magazines.
- Do not feel that you must be the one to make decisions all the time, allow pupils to have some say in the way they learn.
- Help pupils with some of the daily tasks such as tidying books and cupboards or clearing up after a messy activity.

Attitudes towards pupils

Research on the quality of teaching shows that teachers understand the importance of developing self-confidence and self-esteem in their pupils. You will find that your pupils make more progress when they feel that you care about them as individuals, and value what they do and feel.

Positive steps to take

- Take a personal interest in each child in your class. Make sure you learn their names as soon as possible at the beginning of the year. Pupils in class 1 or 2 might bring cards for a birthday board, or pictures of parents, brothers or sisters.
- Keep records of particular areas of difficulty for each pupil and learn to share this knowledge with the pupil (see Assessing pupils' progress and achievement, Topic 60).
- Give positive help by remembering to talk about pupils' achievements.
- Find something to praise first before pointing out mistakes. Give marks for sections of an answer that are correct even if the end answer is wrong.
- Really listen to what pupils have to say. Ask them to suggest ideas and make sure that you use these in your lessons. Encourage them to bring things that interest them to school.
- Display pupils' work regularly. Make sure that everyone has an opportunity to show some of their work at some time during the term.

Avoid giving the wrong impression

- Your expressions and body language can give the impression that you do not have time to waste listening to pupils.
- You may not realise that you make some pupils feel that you do not expect good work or the correct answer from them.
- Don't assume that a particular pupil will always be lazy, dull or a trouble-maker.
- Don't allow some pupils to answer questions more frequently than others.
- Don't make fun of answers that are incorrect.
- Don't ask boys first (see Being gender aware and fair, Topic 6).
- Don't be sarcastic or make comparisons with older brothers and sisters.

The hidden curriculum

Traditionally it was thought that learning in school came only from the subjects the pupils studied as part of the syllabus. Now we know that pupils also learn from messages or signals that they pick up from the attitudes of their teachers and other pupils. These make up the hidden curriculum.

Which of the following statements fits your attitude towards your pupils best?

1 I need to be in charge and expect to make the decisions in the class.

2 Pupils learn more if they are allowed to find things out for themselves.

3 Young children need guidance – they cannot make decisions for themselves until they are shown the right way. That is the teacher's job.

4 I want pupils to be independent and to learn how to make decisions themselves.

5 The pupils in my class would do much better if they made more effort.

6 Finding something to praise builds confidence and even poor students try a little harder.

7 Pupils do not respect teachers as they did when I was in school. If I am not strict they won't learn anything.

8 I like my pupils to treat me as a friend. If they cannot understand the lesson I like to feel they will not be afraid to ask for an explanation.

Which give a more positive view of the learning of your pupils?

Positive attitudes

It is important to let your pupils know that the **process** of learning (the way they learn) is just as important as the **outcome** (the marks that they get).

3 Teaching skills

The skills I use as a teacher

- Organising
- Observing pupils
- Planning
- Assessing progress
- Managing
- Communicating/Listening
- Evaluating my pupils' work
- Monitoring what my pupils are doing

To be a good teacher you need to have a variety of personal and professional skills to help you to teach successfully. You also need to develop ways of improving your teaching.

The skills you need may be general teaching skills like using the chalkboard, or questioning and explaining. They may be more specific skills such as the decisions you make on the choice of materials or ways of teaching a particular subject. Skills can be divided into the following groups.

Organisation (See page 20.)

- Organising the classroom to make the best use of space.
- Providing clear rules and routines.
- Keeping pupils working actively.

Planning (See page 32.)

- Making sure that the syllabus is properly covered.
- Thinking about the best the way to present your lesson.
- Making provision for children working at different levels.
- Providing a variety of activities – listening/oral/written and practical work.

Management (See page 42.)

- Class control.
- Time management.
- The management of both group and individual learning.
- Management of teaching resources by making the most of local materials.

Communication (See pages 136–139.)

- Questioning and explaining new ideas.
- Your relations with pupils.
- Relations with other staff.
- Relations with parents.

Monitoring (See pages 120–125.)

- **Observation** Dealing with more than one thing at once. Knowing exactly what is going on in the class even when your back is turned or you are attending to the needs of another pupil. Ask yourself, **Is everyone paying attention?**
- **Assessing progress** Judging the progress and learning achievement of all pupils.
  Ask yourself, **Do all the pupils understand what needs to be done?**
  Is anyone having difficulties?

Activity *My levels of skill*

Evaluate your level of expertise in each of the skills by grading yourself as **good, satisfactory** or **needs to be developed**.

You might, for example, feel confident about your class control and award yourself with a **good**. Perhaps you are less confident about the way that you handle group work and feel that your skills in that area **need to be developed.**

Evaluation

- Evaluating the learning achievement of pupils through questions, written work and tests.
- Practising self-reflection (the ability to honestly evaluate the strengths and weakness of your own teaching).

Developing your skills

Evaluation helps to improve your teaching and the pupils' learning.

Stage 1 Observation

Develop an awareness of the teaching skills you need and an understanding of how they will make your teaching better. Make notes identifying the areas of strength and weakness in your lesson. Try to find time to watch other teachers and share ideas with them (see Working with other staff, Topic 66).

Stage 2 Practice

Teaching skills improve with practice. Most teachers develop many different special skills as they work in their classrooms. Sometimes you will be able to practise particular skills, e.g. group work skills, during in-service workshops. Find opportunities to share your new knowledge with other members of staff.

Stage 3 Evaluation

This can range from your own feeling that the lesson went well to a detailed feedback given by observers (an inspector, the head, other teachers or pupils). An evaluation that helps you to recognise your strengths and weaknesses will help you change and improve your performance. (See also Evaluating your performance, Topic 8).

4 The process of learning

Useful Definitions

Cognitive strategies processes that pupils use in order to learn, e.g. paying attention, thinking, memorising and solving problems.

Attitudes feelings a pupil may have towards learning certain subjects or learning in a certain way that can influence his or her motivation and ability to think and learn. For example, many pupils think Maths is hard and therefore, feel they cannot do it.

Receptive learning is teacher-centred, that is the teacher uses a lecture method to present the content of the lesson to the learner.

Discovery learning requires pupils to find out answers for themselves through a series of activities. They observe, collect information and then use what they have learned to answer questions.

Meaningful activities/ learning activities and learning that can be related to what the learner already knows and to real-life situations.

Rote learning learning by heart.

Reinforcement improving understanding by building on previous knowledge or repeating information in a different way.

Unless you understand how, why and when your pupils are learning it is impossible to improve your teaching and achieve higher levels of learning in your class.

How do you know when pupils are learning?

Effective teaching involves getting all of these conditions right.

- Pupils must be concentrating and paying attention.
- Pupils must be motivated, ready and willing to learn.
- The learning must be at the right level and related to their knowledge and understanding.
- Pupils should be actively involved in the task and with each other.
- Pupils should be interested in and enjoying the subject.

Why do pupils learn?

- Pupils may be interested in the subject/topic and want to know more.
- The teacher enjoys teaching the subject and is able to arouse curiosity and interest.
- Pupils have to learn the subject in order to pass tests and exams or get to secondary school.

Styles of learning

We all feel more confident about learning when at least some of the material is presented in the way we like best.

The ideal learning situation needs to make use of a variety of strategies, such as:

- Spoken information.
- Supporting teaching and visual aids.
- Practical activities.
- Opportunities for discussion both teacher/pupil and pupil/pupil.
- Time for thinking and reflection.

What processes are involved when pupils are learning?

Cognitive strategies (Ways of learning)

- Receiving information: concentrating, paying attention, selection
- Processing information: conscious thinking and memorising **(short term memory)**
- Storage and retrieval: provides evidence of learning by recalling and using information for problem solving **(long term memory)**

Promoting effective learning. What is the role of the teacher?

Q How can I get my pupils to concentrate?

A Aim to get high levels of attentiveness and concentration.

- Plan the presentation of each lesson carefully.
- Provide a variety of learning activities that actively involve pupils.

Q How can I encourage learning and make it something they want to do?

A Make use of various types of motivation.

- Create a learning environment in the classroom, rousing curiosity and offering opportunities for success.
- Make use of pupils' own interest and motivation.

Q How can I make sure that my lessons are appropriate for the age and ability of my pupils?

A Match the learning to each pupil's existing knowledge and understanding.

- Provide information and activities that relate to your pupils' experience.
- Monitor progress through observation, questions and tests. You can then identify where certain pupils are finding the work difficult and be in a better position to give help.

What's my style

Not everyone learns in the same way. Which of the comments below describes your own style of learning best?

- Doing a practical activity helps me remember what I have learned.
- I need to see something written down.
- If I feel that I can use the information in some way, I can remember it more easily.
- I like to have time to think about what I have heard or learned.

Activity *Thinking about pupil motivation*

(This is also useful as an activity to build up knowledge about individual pupils (see Observation, Topic 60.).

- My pupils seem to learn more quickly **when** they ...
- They seem to learn more slowly **when** they ...
- Ask yourself, **How do I know? How can I get this information?**

Activity *Thinking about teaching methods*

1 Pupils in my class seem to learn best **when** I ...

(for example) start a new topic by bringing something interesting to the class.

2 Can you identify particular pupils who seem to learn most effectively from:

- working on their own?
- group activities?
- books?
- practical activities?

Ask yourself, **How do I know?/How can I get this information?**

What motivates my class?

- My class works well in [name of subjects] because . . . . .
- My pupils like [name of subjects] least. This is because . . . . .

Is there any relationship between your answer here and the one you gave in the activity in Topic 1, Knowledge?

Activity *Identifying your pupils' learning styles*

Think about individual pupils in your class. List the pupils who prefer each of the following styles.

Learning by **touching**

Learning by **doing**

Learning by **reading**

Learning by **seeing**

Learning by **listening**

Learning by **writing**

5 Language policy

Activity *What languages do your pupils speak?*

What is the language of instruction (the local language) in your school?

- Make a list of the different languages spoken by pupils in your class.
- How many of your pupils speak the local language as their mother tongue (the language spoken by **both** parents)?
- How many of your pupils belong to households where the mother and father speak different though perhaps related dialects or languages?
- How many of your pupils come from a language area entirely different to the one where the school is located?

Activity *What language should I use?*

- Is your language the same as that taught in the local area?
- How many of your pupils can speak a local language but cannot read or write it?
- Are lower primary textbooks written in English or the local language?
- Have you any supplementary books in the local language?
- Which subjects are difficult to teach in the local language?
- Use both languages together in your teaching.

There are two main reasons why language specialists believe that young children should be taught in their own language. Which do you think is the most important?

- If pupils learn in a foreign language such as English, they may begin to feel that their own language and culture is less important than the foreign language and ideas they learn in school.
- Pupils learn ideas more easily and thoroughly when they are taught in their mother tongue.

The language policy in primary schools follows a very similar pattern in many African countries. Pupils are taught in the local language in lower primary classes (1–3) and in English or another foreign language (such as French, Spanish or Portuguese) in the upper primary classes (4–6) and in Junior Secondary schools. There are, however, a number of problems relating to this policy that you will have to face.

As you take time to think about these questions you will realise that language is a very complicated issue. In order to solve some of the problems a few countries have adopted a common language that is spoken and understood across a large area, e.g. Hausa, Swahili or Setswana. In others there may be a number of official languages spoken in different regions of the country. As a result many of your pupils probably speak one language at home but are taught in a quite different local language in your school.

Teaching in the local language

The questions in the activity focus on some of the problems faced by teachers. You may find yourself teaching in an area where you do not speak the official local language fluently. There may be new pupils in your class whose parents have been posted to your area who cannot speak or understand the language taught in your school.

What should I do if I cannot speak the child's language?

Should I:

- Speak the local language and hope that the child will gradually begin to understand?
- Find another local language that you both understand?
- Find someone in the class who can speak the child's language and who can translate for you?
- Speak in English?

> ***Activity*** *What do I do if I am unable to speak the local language fluently or if the textbooks are written in English?*
>
> Should I:
>
> - Teach in English and get a pupil to translate difficult ideas for you.
> - Pair pupils so that one who can understand some English translates for his/her partner.

> ***Activity*** *Learning in a second language*
>
> - What methods does your ministry recommend you to use when changing from teaching in the local language to teaching in English? What problems do you face?
> - Are you allowed to use both languages together for a while?
> - How do you explain the meaning of new words or ideas?

Which subjects are most difficult to translate into the local language?

Science, and Mathematics are usually the most difficult. Some words or expressions used in English, for example, may be equally difficult to translate.

Changing from the local language into English

Many teachers find that it is difficult to get pupils to change from one language to another. One method used fairly successfully is to first concentrate on the spoken language.

Developing oral work

You may have noticed that your pupils talk quite fluently to each other in more than one local language. Build on this ability to develop fluency in local languages and in English. This is an opportunity to use story telling, drama or mime. (See Using stories in lessons, Topic 42 and Drama, mime and role-play, Topic 47.)

Begin your language lesson by telling a short story. This may be in the local language in lower primary classes or in English in classes 4 to 6. Develop language skills through:

- **Dramatic activities** Divide your class into three groups. Group 1 can think about the characters in your story and make up a short play about them. Group 2 can mime some of the words or actions and Group 3 can retell the story in the second language.
- **Conversation exercises** Use the story for conversation activities:
  - ask and answer questions.
  - explain something about the story.
  - discuss a particular theme from the story.

Try to involve all your pupils. You can monitor their conversations by moving around the room listening to them talk to each other. (See Children talking to each other, Topic 26.).

6 Being gender aware and fair

Useful definitions

- **Sex** being biologically male or female.
- **Gender** the social and cultural roles which we give to the different sexes.
- **Stereotypes** shared beliefs about people in a particular group. They are not based on fact. For example: 'taxi drivers are dishonest'.
- **Gender stereotypes** shared beliefs about the work roles or behaviour of men and women. For example: 'men are better drivers than women' or 'a woman's place is in the home'.
- **Gender bias** attitudes and practices which show gender stereotypes. For example showing one gender, either boys or girls, as always in the lead, active, successful and valued.
- **Positive role models** a role model is someone that you admire. When choosing a career children may model themselves on someone who has done well. It is important for girls to know about women who have succeeded in their careers as doctors, scientists, traders, farmers, etc.
- **Gender fairness** believing that boys and girls have equal value. Making sure that they have equal opportunities to learn and to take responsibility.

Most governments are trying to provide equal opportunities in education. But boys and girls are still not always treated equally.

In lower primary classes girls often do as well as, or better than boys. But as they get older girls often have poorer attendance and may drop out of school early. Girls' secondary school exam results in Maths, Science and Technical subjects are usually lower than boys'. There may be several reasons for the differences.

- The curriculum is more suitable for boys.
- Girls do less well in Mathematics and Science at primary level.
- Textbooks and other educational materials contain gender stereotypes.
- Girls lack positive role models.
- Girls are not always encouraged to do well in school by either teachers or parents.

How does this affect your teaching?

There are three main ways in which gender bias can affect the education of boys or girls. As a teacher, you need to be aware of these.

1 Bias in textbooks

Are the books you use 'gender sensitive'? Do they show roles and attitudes for both men and women that are no longer true or realistic? The impressions gained from biased textbooks and stories can have a lasting effect on the attitudes of both boys and girls. Many countries are now beginning to produce textbooks that provide a more balanced view.

What is wrong with this picture?

Activity *Check for bias in classroom*

Are girls and boys separated on the class register? Is this really necessary?

- Do boys and girls sit in separate groups?
- Do they march in separate groups to assembly or to another class?
- Do boys and girls have an equal chance to be a class monitor?
- Do you expect girls to be as good at Maths and Science as boys?
- Do you expect boys to help equally with classroom chores?
- Do you encourage both girls and boys to be serious about their education?
- Do you use biased language, e.g. 'Kweku is behaving like a girl' or 'The boys are stronger, they can clear away the chairs'?

Activity *Check the textbooks you use for gender bias*

- Is there a balance in the number of men and women in the text and in illustrations?
- Look at the roles of boys and girls.

  Are boys/men shown as: active, able to give advice and guidance, the head of the household, holding important jobs?

  Are girls/women shown as: housewives, helpers, seeking advice or needing help?

  Are men shown in jobs such as: pilot, driver, doctor, architect?

  Are women usually shown in jobs such as: housewife, nurse, secretary?

Things to do

Family roles

Look at this picture. Which activities can be done by men? Which activities can be done by women?

- Make a chart to show how work and daily tasks are divided between men and women in your community.
- Are **roles** changing?

Activity *Suggestions for changes*

1. Change seating and groups regularly.
2. Let boys and girls take responsibility for tasks in turn.
3. Learn to use impersonal words: principal or headteacher rather than headmaster, police officer not policeman.
4. Find stories about famous women that pupils can read or dramatise.
5. Include in the curriculum items which show women playing important roles, e.g. in current events.

2 Parent and pupil bias

In many societies certain tasks are given to boys and girls from their earliest years. This results in differences in their up-bringing. Girls are usually expected to do household tasks and look after younger brothers and sisters. Boys often have greater freedom.

These differences affect the choices pupils make about school subjects or their roles. Differences may not be so obvious in lower primary classes but may appear as pupils get older.

- Girls may become less keen to answer questions first.
- Boys may be less willing to take part in cleaning activities.
- Girls may be reluctant to take the lead in practical activities.

3 Teacher bias

Teachers may assume that girls are better suited to do Arts and Language subjects than boys, or that boys are better able to do Maths and Science than girls. Teachers often unconsciously use gender to manage pupils in their classes. Teachers may also give more attention to boys, asking them questions, and disciplining them.

7 Reflection

Daily Before you leave school. Try to find some time to think about the lessons you have given that day (see 'Evaluating your performance, Topic 8).

Weekly Once a week, perhaps during the lunch break, you might arrange to meet colleagues and think about issues that have cropped up during the previous week. (See Working with other staff, Topic 66).

As part of teacher appraisal
Some schools have now introduced a process of teacher appraisal. This process should give you a valuable opportunity to reflect on your teaching as you talk to the head or senior teacher.

Improving your teaching skills is a life-long process.

Why do we need to reflect on the way we teach?

Reflection is a process of self-appraisal or self-evaluation that allows you to think about your teaching skills and practice. Begin with an evaluation of the strengths and weaknesses of your teaching. (Look at Teaching skills, Topic 3.) One method of looking at yourself as a teacher is to carry out a **SWOT** analysis. The example shows how this is done and the way one teacher assessed herself.

S (Strengths)	**W (Weaknesses)**
My curriculum knowledge is generally good. *My knowledge of the local area is good and can be used in lessons.* *I still enjoy teaching despite the difficulties.*	*I tend to give too much written information in lessons.* *I am not always sure of individual learning difficulties.*
O (Opportunities)	**T (Threats)**
I could study a new teacher's manual that has been sent to the school. *The head has suggested that we should hold a meeting to plan improvements in the teaching of reading next year.*	*Finding time to carry out all the activities necessary to prepare lessons and assess pupils properly.*

When and how should reflection be done?

Reflection should be an on-going activity. Making notes on each lesson in your record book can be very useful. It can be done alone, with colleagues or as part of an appraisal process.

How can reflection improve the quality of teaching and learning in my class?

Look at the SWOT analysis. You need to think about overcoming the areas of weakness and finding a way of eliminating the threats. Reflection can improve your teaching if you take time to do it.

- What do you need to learn in order to improve the content of lessons or the approach to topics?
- What changes do you need to make before giving other lessons on a similar topic?

- What methods might you need to change in order to improve learning and motivation?
- How could you improve the timing of your lessons?
- What kind of support might you need (from the school or in-service programmes) to help you sustain improvement?

The example of a SWOT analysis showed two areas of weakness and one area of threat.

On reflection he/she might involve pupils in more activities and instead of filling the board with notes ask them to write their own notes, using key words or headings.

- The teacher felt that he/she gave too much written information in lessons.

On reflection, he/she might plan to make a more detailed observation of each pupil in order to find specific areas of weakness. (See Assessing pupils' progress and achievement, Topic 60.)

- The teacher felt unsure of the learning difficulties of individual pupils.

This can be a problem for all primary teachers. Many do not have free periods during the day and transport difficulties may leave little or no time to plan after school. Nevertheless, it is possible to make better use of the time available. (See Time management, Topic 21.) Plan to make a more systematic observation of pupils during lessons and arrange to work on lesson plans after school, one afternoon each week, perhaps with a colleague.

- The teacher felt threatened by the difficulty of finding enough time to carry out all the activities necessary.

Remember there is only so much you can do on your own. Your teaching skills will develop best where you work with other teachers or student teachers who are willing to share their experiences and where your headteacher or tutor provides support by encouraging staff to share problems and develop new ideas.

8 Evaluating my performance

We all need to evaluate our own performance from time to time in order to identify our strengths and weaknesses and work towards improving our teaching skills. Your Ministry may also use performance evaluation – Teacher Performance Appraisal – for the purpose of promotion so it is useful to have thought carefully about your own skills.

These checklists are designed to help you evaluate your teaching performance. In this topic each checklist looks at particular skills – Planning, performance, classroom management and communication skills. Add your own ideas to the checklists as there are a number of different areas that you might feel are important to evaluate.

Concentrate on one section at a time for a period of a week. Read through each section carefully and make a note of your own comments. After each evaluation make a list of Targets you need to develop and where you might find help.

You can use the record opposite to help you.

How effective was my planning?

1 Did I identify the objectives and core points clearly?
2 What teaching aids did I use?
3 What other resources could have been used?
4 Did I use the right method and activities for the lesson?
5 Were the activities done successfully by the pupils?
6 Was the timing right?
7 Did I achieve the objectives?

How effective was my performance?

1 Were all my resources suitable?
2 Is my voice clear and audible?
3 Were questions/explanations too easy or too hard?
4 Is my board work clear and legible?
5 Did I give instructions clearly?
6 Did I supervise tasks/activities properly?
7 Did I encourage pupils to think about the work and listen to their answers?
8 Was I able to identify pupils who had difficulty with the lesson?
9 Do I have extra tasks for those who finish their work quickly?
10 Did I end the lesson on time?
11 Did all pupils finish the tasks?
12 Did the class enjoy the lesson?

Activity *Evaluation of my teaching skills*

Areas to improve:

e.g.
Identifying particular learning difficulties of my pupils

My targets

1 Keep more systematic records of each child (see Topic 9 Guidance and counselling and Topic 35 Helping individual pupils).

2 Provide a greater variety of learning activities (Topic 29 Successful learning).

Who can help me?

Other teachers who have taught those pupils

The head or local education officer

Other sections of this book that might help.

How effective was my classroom management?

1 Have I made the best use of classroom space?
2 Have I made good use of display areas?
3 Have I kept pupils busy?
4 Have I looked at the work in all groups at some time during the lesson?
5 Have I avoided a queue of children at my desk?
6 Have I carried out a weekly check to make sure all pupils have completed assignments, homework and other tasks?
7 Have I been able to anticipate and control disruptive behaviour?

How effective are my communication skills?

1 Do I react unfairly or too harshly or am I too lenient?
2 Have I worked out a way of getting difficult pupils to work on worthwhile tasks?
3 Do I avoid using sarcastic or humiliating remarks?
4 Do I try to develop thinking?
5 Am I a good listener?
6 Do my pupils feel that I enjoy teaching them?
7 Have I remembered to avoid gender bias?

IMPROVE *teaching and learning in your class!*

***I**nterest*	*pupils by making lessons stimulating and enjoyable.*
***M**otivate*	*by giving positive help and praise.*
***P**lan*	*a variety of methods and activities that involve pupils in their own learning.*
***R**einforce*	*learning by building on existing knowledge and understanding and linking it to new knowledge.*
***O**ffer*	*opportunities for success.*
***V**erify*	*How much pupils have learned by monitoring progress.*
***E**valuate*	*Your performance through observation and reflection.*

9 Guidance and counselling

Activity *Noting problems*

Which of the following problems have you noted? (They may apply to either boys or girls.)

- One of my pupils missed more than ten days of school last term.
- Some pupils always seem tired.
- One or two of the bigger pupils bully the younger or smaller members of the class.
- Some pupils are so nervous in the term examinations that they are unable to complete the questions properly.
- Last year several of my pupils were unable to gain entrance into Senior Secondary School.
- I think some of my pupils are getting into bad company.
- I suspect that there is someone in my class who vandalises material that we have put on display.
- A new pupil in my class is having great difficulty making friends.

Are there any other more serious problems that you have had to face that require skills in guidance and counselling such as early pregnancies, HIV/Aids or drugs?

As a class teacher you are responsible not only for the academic progress of your pupils but also for their social and emotional welfare. Very few primary teachers are given training in counselling and yet and in almost every primary class there are a few pupils who will need help at some time. The first activity in this topic outlines a number of common problems which may affect the behaviour and progress of your pupils.

Your school may have guidelines to help deal with more serious problems but there will be other issues that you can resolve by providing the kind of atmosphere in your class that encourages your pupils to talk about their concerns.

What skills do you need to be a good counsellor?

Two skills are particularly important: awareness and being a good listener.

Awareness

You need to be constantly aware of things that might affect your pupils both in the classroom and outside. Bullying, for example, is more likely to take place during the breaks or after school than it is in your classroom.

Being a good listener

Being able to talk to a teacher is often a great help to pupils, even if you cannot solve their problems.

You will need to be a good listener. Children are often reluctant to talk about themselves to an adult. Unfortunately as teachers or parents we often take a leading role and tell children what they have done wrong and how they must behave. You need to learn to listen to what your pupils want to say without interrupting them or telling them what *you* think.

Be a friend as well as a teacher

Your pupils need to feel that you are there to help them. Without making it seem as if you are prying into their personal life, try to find a way of talking to each child about schoolwork, hobbies, their likes and dislikes or their ideas about a future career. If you want your pupils to confide in you, you must show that you are interested in them and be willing to share some of your experiences.

> ***Activity*** *Getting to know your pupils*
>
> In order to help individual pupils, you will need to have some idea of the family background of each child.
>
> - Is he/she living with parents, grandparents or guardians?
> - Does he/she live near the school?
> - What is the occupation of his/her parents?
> - Are older or younger brothers or sisters in other classes in the school, or in other schools?
> - Does the child have any health problems that you should know about?
>
> This information may be recorded by the headteacher when the child first enrols in your school. Make sure that you have read whatever records are available but remember this is only the beginning of learning about your pupils.

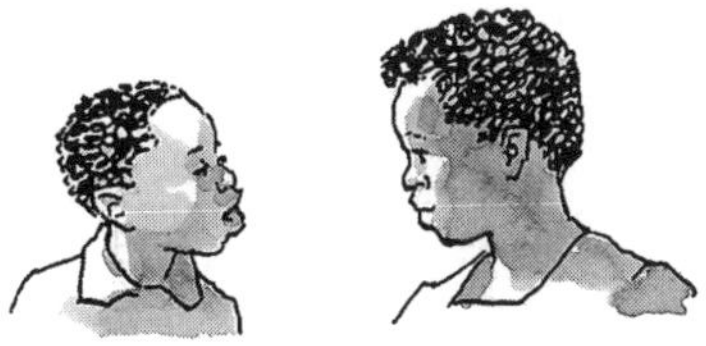

Help your pupils to have confidence in their ability to succeed

It has been found that success in school is often as closely related to feelings of self-esteem and confidence in pupils as it is to their academic ability. It has also been found that where teachers show that they believe that their pupils will succeed, even those with very little academic ability respond in a more positive way. (See also Praise and punishment, Topic 30.)

How can you help?

There are some simple actions that you can take to give your pupils confidence.

- Never make fun of someone who answers a question wrongly or who does not seem to have understood the lesson. Encourage pupils to ask questions. You may find that others have not understood that part very well either. It may be that you did not explain it clearly. Suggest that you could go through it again for everyone.
- Help pupils who have missed school. When they return to class show them the topics they have missed. Keep notes of lesson activities so that they can go through them in their own time. If you do not have as much time as you would like, suggest that they should work with another member of the class. They can talk to you again if there is something they still do not understand.
- Offer support to pupils who have failed an important examination. Go over key topics again for those who did not understand the first time and help pupils see 'what went wrong'. You might also use the pairing technique. (See Remedial teaching, Topic 38 and Working in pairs, Topic 34.)

Dealing with problems

The way you decide to deal with problems will be based on your knowledge of your pupils and the situation.

- In some cases, particularly where your pupil has a personal problem he/she may respond more positively if you arrange to talk privately after school. This is the **individual interview** technique.
- Other issues may be dealt with more effectively in a group. As long as no one's name is mentioned you may find it better to raise issues like bullying or vandalism as a general topic. This is the **group discussion** technique.

Whichever method you use, always let pupils know that you are there to help, not to judge.

10 Organising your classroom

Activity *Making changes to your classroom*

Take a few moments to look at your classroom.

- How many children are in your class? What is the best way to seat them?
- Can the walls be used to display teaching aids and children's work? (See Displaying pupils' work, Topic 55.)
- How easy is it to rearrange the furniture?
- Is the teacher's desk in the best place?
- Can the pupils use any of the floor space for sitting or working?
- Can you move around easily?
- Can all the pupils see the chalkboard? Can they see and hear you?
- Are pupils who need special help seated near you?

What changes can be made to improve the classroom?

Even in a school with very few resources, a good teacher can create a well-ordered classroom that encourages learning.

What encourages learning in this class?

Curriculum areas

Arrange curriculum areas in different parts of the room.

- A reading corner for story time, and quiet reading.
- A Nature/Science table, for displaying collections and experiments.
- Subject display areas, with simple teaching aids and displays of work.

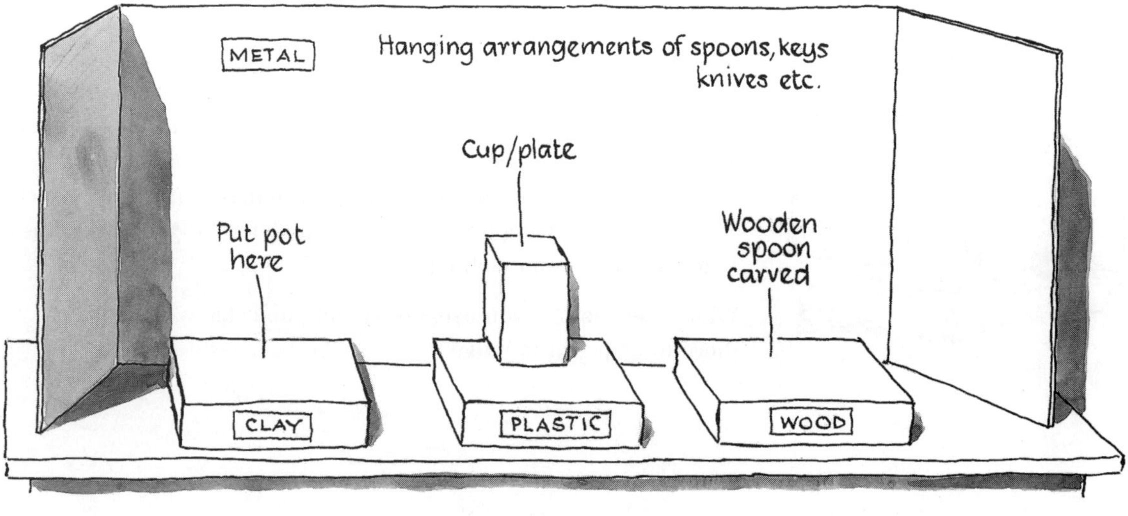

Change the displays regularly, at least once a term. Use these areas as a focus for some lessons, instead of the chalkboard.

Activity *Making best use of space*

- Make a list of the different kinds of activities you may want to do with pupils in an average term.
- **Either** try different classroom arrangements out in practice over the next term;

or make a small scale plan of your classroom (3 cm: 1m, or 1 thumb length to 3 paces).

- Make paper cut-outs for the pieces of furniture that are in the room. Try rearranging the paper cut outs to suit different activities. Then try them out in practice.
- Do not try to rearrange your classroom when all the pupils are in it. This is likely to be noisy and could cause a disturbance. Ask a small group of pupils to help you at the beginning or end of the day.

Seating arrangements

Who decides where the children will sit? Is the seating arrangement fair to both boys and girls? (See Being gender aware and fair, Topic 6.)

Do not use the same seating arrangement all the time. Straight rows are useful but groups can be more flexible. If classes are not too large it may be possible to rearrange the groups for different lessons. (See the diagram opposite and Group work, Topic 33.) Groups of pupils can focus on curriculum areas. They are also useful when learning materials have to be shared. Different arrangements can be helpful for different activities, for example: art, drama, projects, subject lessons, classwork, group work, pair work and individual work.

What if there are more children than desks?

If there are too few desks, do not crowd children together with three or more at one desk. Place the desks along the wall and sit the children in groups on the floor. The desks can then be used for writing activities when needed. Not all groups need to write at the same time.

What if you have to teach outside?

Choose your area carefully, perhaps near a large tree or a wall that will provide shade and a focus point. It is usually better to sit pupils in groups rather than in a large circle or in straight lines. The space in the middle of a large circle distances the pupils from you and it will be more difficult to maintain eye contact with everyone in the class. For some subjects, such as drama, the space you have outside can be a positive advantage.

11 Making your classroom interesting to work in

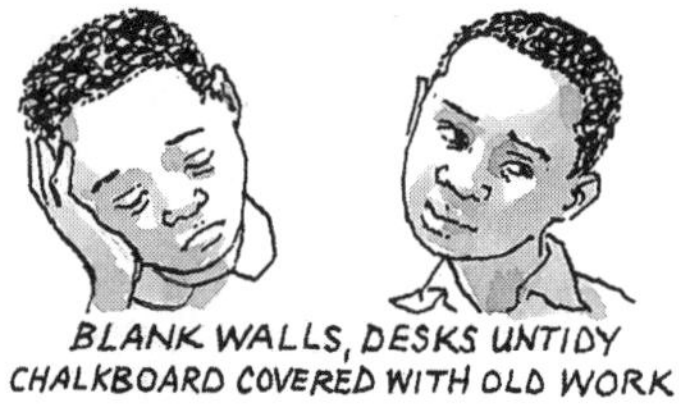

Activity

What do you mean by **interesting?** The dictionary suggests: *stimulating, attractive, exciting, absorbing.* Would a visitor to the school choose one of these words to describe your classroom and lessons?

Is this your classroom?

Organising your classroom, Topic 10 shows a classroom can easily be divided into interest areas with reading, science and nature areas and displays of pupils' work on the walls. Even if you have few resources you can make your classroom an interesting and pleasant place to work in.

Example Recycling

A water filter can be made from a recycled plastic bottle and would be useful in the home.

They will need:

A large plastic bottle cut in half,

Some cotton (kapok or cotton lint),

Some fine sand and gravel.

(See also Topic 41, Experiments and demonstrations.)

Make your classroom part of the learning environment

What creates interest and excitement in a classroom? The Section on Resources shows the importance of providing teaching aids or using models and apparatus and displays to improve learning. These resources will quickly become boring if you do not vary the methods you use to keep the interest of your pupils.

Make changes to the displays regularly. If you are about to start a new topic on a particular theme, e.g. 'Our Community' (see Managing large classes, Topic 13), you can prepare the display area by putting up questions on flashcards: What do we need? Where shall we start? Involve the pupils in making more question flashcards.

Discuss a display that your pupils have to make on their own. Lessons on the environment may lead to looking at **Recycling**. A local study of the great variety of ways that people re-use materials such as newspaper, rubber tyres, plastic bottles and bags, or rope and string could lead to other topics in subjects like Maths, Technology, Art or Craft. Pupils could design or make useful objects using recycled materials themselves.

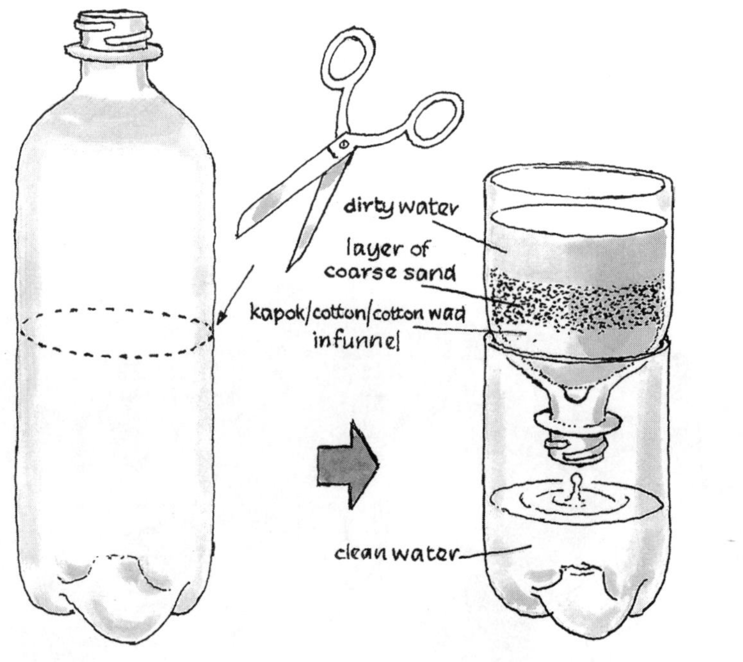

A water filter

Activity *Using displays in your lessons*

- Refer to the display regularly, during lessons.
- Leave spaces for pupils to make labels or to contribute their own information and ideas.
- Add a **Find out** section. You can give merit points to the group that finds out the answer first.
- You can offer to provide the background for their display. Encourage the pupils to bring in as much material as possible themselves.

A news board or information corner

Sometimes pupils want to tell others about an interesting event they have experienced but there may not be an appropriate time for this activity in the syllabus. Leave a space on the wall (or you might use the back of the door) labelled **News** and allow the pupils to make their own display. Make sure there are sensible guidelines, made after discussion with the whole class. Use opportunities to comment on particularly interesting and unusual items of news or displays. This could lead to a class newspaper and involve other areas of the curriculum.

What makes you an interesting teacher?

The provision of interesting and stimulating resource materials is not the only way to make your classroom an interesting place to work in. A lot may depend on you, the way you present your lessons and your relationship with your pupils.

Interesting teachers are not necessarily those who are the most clever. They are more likely to be the ones who genuinely like their pupils and enjoy presenting the lesson in a slightly unusual way. They can also link the lesson to something that pupils know, make their pupils think and get a discussion started.

Activity *Interesting teachers*

Think about a teacher whose class you always enjoyed. What was special about him/her?

What do your pupils think of you?

- Do they think you are too strict?
- Do they think you are easy going?
- Are you difficult to talk to or can you always find time to listen to your pupils?
- Do your lessons always follow the same pattern?
- Do your pupils know how you want them to behave and work?
- Do you allow times for fun and creativity?
- Is there a special time each week when they know there will be something unusual to do?

12 Mixed-ability and mixed-age classes

Definitions

Mixed-ability classes

Even within the same age group, pupils learn in different ways and at a different pace. Some teachers believe that pupils learn best when they can share their learning and experience. They feel that pupils benefit more if there is a mixed range of ability in the class.

Mixed-age classes

A class is classified as mixed-age where the age range is larger than the normal.

Activity *Finding different tasks*

- In the groups, make sure that responsibilities are shared between brighter pupils and those who are less able, or between older and younger members of the class.
- Grade tasks so that even the weakest or youngest pupil can complete a minimum number of tasks accurately.

Resources

- Mixed-ability, mixed-age groups will need more than the basic textbook.
- Groups will need access to reference material.
- Have a variety of activities from fact-finding, to imaginative and creative work catering for the full range of abilities.
- Gradually build up a work folder of variety of activities and tasks on different topics.
- Model your ideas on resources available in your school or at the local Teachers' Resource Centre.

There are several ways in which pupils are assigned to class groups when they first enter a school. In some large schools they are 'streamed' – placed in different classes according to their ability. Other schools place pupils in mixed-ability groups and in some cases in mixed-age groups.

In Africa, mixed-age classes are common. In remote, rural schools the head may have to combine two or even three classes especially where:

- There are very few pupils in some year groups.
- There are serious staff shortages.

Not all pupils are able to start primary school at the prescribed age. There could be three or more years difference between the oldest and the youngest member of any class in a primary school. Some may be enrolled into Class 1 at six, whilst others may not begin until they are eight or even nine years old. The system of repeating a year's work also increases the age range, particularly in the upper primary classes.

A wide range of age or ability within a class will affect both the way that material is presented by the teacher and the type of activities that pupils can do.

Teaching mixed-ability or mixed-age classes – the role of the teacher

You need to prepare activities for the full range of learning needs in the class.

- Many of your lessons will need to be more informal with pupils/groups working on different activities at their own pace. (See Group work, Topic 33 and Project work, Topic 48.). In schools where there are few resources and large classes this can be very difficult.
- Try to find time to work with other teachers (see Working with other staff, Topic 66) in order to prepare a greater variety of activities. (See Making learning active, Topic 25.)

Classroom organisation

Mixed-ability classes

Even where classes have a normal age range pupils usually have a range of ability.

For some subjects such as English or Mathematics you will probably group pupils according to their ability. That way it will be easier for you to provide activities that suit the learning needs of each group.

> ***Activity*** *Finding activities for mixed-age/mixed-ability groups*
>
> See Water (Topic 48), Working with the community (Topic 69) or the Newspaper project (Project Work, Topic 48.)
>
> Study each section carefully and decide which section/s might be used during the introductory lessons. Remember, the whole class needs to be involved in the introduction, so choose something that is interesting and can be understood by a range of pupils.
>
> Look at the activities in each subject area. Which ones can be achieved by the majority of pupils? Which ones are more suitable for very bright (or older) students? Which activities can be adapted for weaker (or the youngest) pupils?

In other subjects such as science or social studies, especially where you are working on a project, ability may not be a major consideration and you can be more flexible. You can allow your pupils to form friendship or interest groups that are not related to their ability.

Try to change your groups around from time to time as it can be very disheartening for a pupil who is always in the bottom group.

Mixed-age classes

Assess your class in terms of ability as well as age. Be flexible in your arrangements.

Where two or more year groups have to be taught together, it may be easier to group pupils in year rather than ability groups. Some topics such as compostion or a study of local history may still be taught to the whole class. Lessons should include a general introduction to the topic followed by different activities suggested in the syllabus for each year group.

The age range may be large because some pupils did not start school at the normal age or may have learning problems. In those circumstances, you can form groups based according to ability rather than age. In Maths, for example, some of the brighter pupils in the younger group may be able to work with older pupils. In composition writing or Environment Studies, however, do not expect the younger pupils to have the same grasp of language skills as the older group. Age groups would be more successful.

Making a lesson plan

If the timetable is fairly flexible, you may need to make use of double periods for some subjects as it takes time to set up a good range of group activities.

The importance of the introduction

This should involve the whole class (See Working with the whole class, Topic 32). It is important to gain the interest and attention of everyone. Give clear instructions about each of the activities.

13 Managing large classes

> ***Activity*** *Teaching large classes*
>
> Add your own problems to the ones listed. You will probably have several that are specific to your school and resources.

In many countries, primary schools normally have classes of 35 to 45 pupils but there are schools where the class size may be double that number. Classes of this size present problems to even the most experienced teachers. What are the problems?

Common problems

Space In large classes there is only a very limited amount of space available for curriculum activity areas or movement and active learning, e.g. role-playing in groups.

The preparation of lesson activities and marking Both of these activities take much longer to do in classes with a large number of pupils.

Resources and learning needs There are rarely enough resources for all pupils/groups in large classes and it is therefore difficult to provide suitable work for the full range of learning needs.

Teaching methods In most primary schools, lessons are fairly short, between 35 and 40 minutes long. Many teachers feel that this does not give enough time to use discovery methods and therefore tend to use more direct teaching methods.

Possible solutions

Think about these ideas in relation to your own school. Can you find any other solutions that might work for your classroom?

Space

There is not a great deal one can do about a lack of space but you might be more creative about seating arrangements or make more use of the playground area for at least one lesson each day. (See Organising your classroom, Topic 10.)

Display areas

A large class puts pressure on display space. Small displays can be mounted on a chair, two desks pushed together, or a few boxes. You might also make more use of the ceiling. (Look at the ideas in Displaying pupils' work, Topic 55.)

Lesson time

Unless there are strict regulations regarding the organisation of the timetable, try to extend some lessons over a double period. You might also try combining topics in different sections of the curriculum into Units of teaching.

Teaching methods

Teaching a large group requires good organisation. You will need to be well prepared so that you have time to monitor and help individuals or groups. If you can, share the preparation of activities and resources with another teacher in the same year group or the teacher in the afternoon shift. (See Working with other staff, Topic 66.) Remember to provide a few activities that can be done easily and at least one that will challenge more able students.

Rotating groups in this way needs practice.

You will need time to develop these skills and your pupils will also need time to learn how to work independently. Always remember to prepare pupils to change activities: 'I want you to stop what you are doing now and move on to the next group.'

Develop a range of self-help strategies for pupils

In order to minimise movement and save time at the beginning and end of lessons, organise routines for giving out and collecting resources and work (See Rules and routines, Topic 14.). This can be done best by a small number of group leaders or a class monitor. Give your pupils training in leadership skills by changing groups and their leaders regularly.

Example *Rotating groups*

Divide the class into three groups (A, B and C). Give groups B and C a simple exercise (one oral and one practical or written exercise) based on the introduction to the lesson. These should not need your attention. Whilst these groups do the exercises, check the understanding of the third group by doing some examples with them on the board. Rotate the groups after eight minutes. During the last eight minutes go over the oral and written activity work that you set at the beginning of the lesson with all the pupils.

Examples *Changing activities*

40 minute lesson plan

Introduction to lesson topic and explanation of group activities (whole class–8 minutes).

Rotated group activities. See the example in the box above (each group – 8 minutes).

Summary of the lesson and review of exercises (whole class–8 minutes).

Activity *Combining topics*

Look through the syllabus and see where you might combine lesson topics from different subjects. Some ideas have been suggested in Project work, Topic 48.

14 Rules and routines

Activity

There are a number of problem areas where it is useful to have rules. In which of these areas do you have rules?

Talking

- Pupils talking to each other.
- Pupils talking to the teacher.
- Silent times.

Time

- Arriving late.
- Wasting time.
- Time to complete tasks.

Pupil-Pupil relationships

- Sharing and working together.
- Fighting.
- Name calling.
- Interference with someone else's work.

Movement

- Standing and sitting.
- Moving around the classroom.
- Entering or leaving the room.
- What to do in an emergency.

Teacher-Pupil relationships

- Obedience.
- Being polite and thoughtful.
- Rudeness.

My rules

Which are the **three or four** most important rules in your classroom?

Why do we need rules?

Making rules is one of the first steps that you will take to establish order in your classroom and create the conditions that encourage pupils to work. (See also Praise and punishment, Topic 30.) Your rules show pupils how they are expected to behave.

How were your rules decided on?

- Did you make your own rules in your classroom?
- Did you discuss and agree on rules with other teachers?
- Do other teachers have the same rules as you?
- Are there clear school rules?

It is a good idea to review rules occasionally. Review your own rules with your pupils and school and classroom rules during staff meetings.

How do your pupils learn about rules?

All school and classroom rules need to be understood by all pupils.

- Do you have some rules displayed in your classroom?
- Do you tell pupils about your important rules at the beginning of the year?
- Do you tell pupils about some rules as the need arises?
- Do you explain **why** you feel certain rules are necessary in your class?

An orderly classroom is achieved by WORKING TOGETHER – don't make your classroom seem threatening.

Encourage pupils to keep rules

1 Be positive

Give reminders

Pupils need time to learn the rules that apply to your classroom and will often need to be reminded of them.

Express rules in a positive way

Avoid a list of 'don'ts'. They tend to act as a challenge to difficult pupils.

Work quietly, rather than, **Don't talk.**

Listen carefully and then you will be able to answer the questions, rather than, **Sit still.**

> **A step by step approach**
>
> **Step 1** **Warning** Remind the pupil that a rule is being broken. In some cases, it is better to ignore small incidents of bad behaviour unless they are affecting the work of others.
>
> **Step 2** **Discussion** Ask him/her to remain in the class during break or after school so that you have an opportunity to talk calmly, away from the rest of the class. Try to identify the cause of the problem. Make clear what action will be taken if the behaviour does not improve. This may include staying in at playtime, writing lines or missing games or some other activity that the pupil usually enjoys.
>
> These steps will usually stop most minor disruptions in the class. Sometimes it may be necessary to take **Step 3.**
>
> **Step 3** **Refer to the head** If the poor behaviour continues, send the pupil to the head. He/she may decide, with you, to ask the parents to be present during an interview. At this stage, more severe punishment may be carried out according to the rules of the school.

Give praise

Praise individuals, groups or the whole class for working quietly or completing a task. (See Praise and punishment, Topic 30.) You may also like to award Stars or Merit points to encourage individual pupils to behave well.

2 Be alert

Be aware of what is happening in the class and try to prevent bad behaviour. Most pupils try to test the teacher's control at some time or another. It is best to prevent trouble if you can by making sure that pupils understand what they have to do and are fully occupied.

3 Take action

There should be clear consequences if rules are broken. The step by step approach illustrated in the box shows a sequence that might be used. (See also the section on Praise and punishment, Topic 30.)

Routines rather than rules

Pupils can often be managed more effectively if **routines** are established for as many activities as possible. Many of the rules mentioned in the activity can be expressed more positively as **routines** rather than **rules.**

Regular classroom routines

You will find it easier to manage your class if you have regular routines for each of the activities listed below.

- Beginning the day: classroom chores, sweeping, organising desks and registration.
- Keeping the classroom tidy: collecting rubbish in a box and putting resource materials away neatly.
- Moving in and out of the classroom.
- The end of the day.
- Beginning a lesson: giving out or collecting homework, books or resources.
- Getting work marked during a lesson.
- Moving from one activity to another.
- Collecting completed assignments.

Work routines might include

- How to work together in a group or in pairs.
- How to talk quietly without disturbing others.
- How to take turns.
- How to work on individual assignments.

Remember to teach your routines to new pupils in your class at the beginning of each year.

15 Coping with problem behaviour

Activity

What are the **four** most common behaviour problems that you cope with each day? Look at the list below. Have you any other problems of your own to add?

- restlessness
- daydreaming
- laziness
- taking other people's pencils or books
- walking in and out of the classroom
- fidgeting
- roaming around the room
- making noises such as humming or tapping
- chatting to neighbours

Much valuable teaching and learning time may be lost correcting bad behaviour. Before you decide on the solution you need to look at the problem objectively.

- What is happening?
- Why is it happening – what is the motive?
- Does the behaviour affect others?

In every class, teachers are faced with problem behaviour of one kind or another. Studies in many different primary schools across Africa show a remarkable similarity in the type of problems that teachers have to deal with.

Is the problem something you can prevent?

Prevention is better than a cure.

You need to be able to keep order in your classroom if your teaching is to be effective. If your lessons are well planned, with a variety of interesting activities, your pupils will have very little time to misbehave.

1 Make sure that all pupils are actively involved in the lesson. Are the activities too hard for pupils with learning difficulties or too easy for very bright pupils?

2 Learn to divide your attention. Give help to an individual or group but stay aware of what is happening elsewhere in the class.

Activity *In what way can these problems affect behaviour in your classroom?*

1 Health problems

- Hunger, malnutrition, malaria, diarrhoea, sickle cell anaemia, slight deafness, poor eyesight.

2 Special needs

- The pupil does not understand the lesson – he/she is a slow learner.
- The pupil is clever but gets bored very quickly.

3 Social or emotional problems

- Difficulties at home.
- Poor relationships with other pupils in the class (bullying, teasing, quarrelling).
- He/she works before/after school on the farm, in the market, doing household chores.

4 Lack of motivation

- The pupil has a long way to walk before and after school.
- No support at home, especially for girls.

5 Teacher/pupil relationships

- The teacher is too strict or too lenient.
- The teacher finds it hard to like the pupil.
- The teacher has made him/her a favourite.

Can you think of other behaviour problems that might affect your class?

3 Talk to parents about health problems and the way they can affect learning.

Noise

You may need to allow a certain level of activity noise. Younger pupils in particular tend to become restless if they are not allowed to move about or if they are expected to remain silent for a long time.

What are your methods?

Some teachers have a way of enforcing rules without seeming to do anything.

There are a number of ways in which teachers can stop problem behaviour before it goes too far:

- Stare at the pupil who is being noisy or not getting on with work.
- Stand silently waiting for attention.
- Touch a pupil lightly on the shoulder without actually saying anything.
- Move towards an individual or a group.
- Make a general remark such as, 'There seems to be a lot of fuss and movement at the moment. I think we all need to settle down.'
- Lower the level of your voice so that pupils have to listen more carefully.

What do you do?

Can you add two or three ways that you use to control a class without punishing anyone?

Actions to avoid

- **Threats:** Some pupils regard a threat as a challenge and they will try to test you. If you do not or cannot carry out the threat it undermines your authority.
- **Arguments:** These often lead to an emotional outburst from the child. If he/she becomes very upset, arrange to talk quietly after the lesson or at break-time. Never allow other children in the class to become involved in the argument.
- **Unfair comparisons:** 'Your brother is much cleverer than you' or 'Class 3B is much better behaved than this group'.
- **Humiliating or insulting remarks:** Once a pupil feels that you do not like him/her you stand very little chance of getting them to work well for you.

16 Preparation and planning

> ***Activity** Preparation and planning*
>
> **What** planning activities do you do and which people do you work with in each of the following?
>
> Long-term schemes of work.
>
> Individual units of work.
>
> Daily lesson planning.
>
> Planning the organisation of your class.
>
> Planning the use of resources and teaching methods.
>
> Preparation of projects, visits or field work.

There are very good reasons for spending time on the careful planning and preparation of your work. It is as important for students/trainees and newly-qualified teachers as it is for more experienced teachers.

- It ensures that you cover all the topics outlined in the syllabus.
- It makes teaching more effective because it focuses on what you want your pupils to learn and how you will achieve that learning.
- It gives you an opportunity to be creative.
- It allows you to make time to monitor the learning process.
- It reduces the likelihood of problems of control when pupil tasks and activities have been planned.

One of the main reasons for planning is that it allows you to organise your material in a way that will interest pupils and provide a variety of activities and tasks suitable for the range of ability in your class.

Planning time

At the beginning of the year, and again at the beginning of each term, most teachers carry out long-term planning and preparation. (See also Schemes of work, Topic 17.) Heads expect more detailed lesson plans to be handed in on a weekly basis. (See Lesson plans,Topic 18 and Lesson presentation skills, Topic 19.) There are, however, a number of other areas that you might consider would benefit from some forward planning.

Long term planning and preparation

What are the things that you need to think about?

- Your subject knowledge in relation to the syllabus.
- The organisation and management of the class.
- The available resources.
- The methods and strategies.
- Assessment

Subject knowledge

Successful teaching and the quality of pupil learning is closely related to the teacher's own knowledge and understanding of a subject. This knowledge needs to be built up gradually over time.

First, check your personal knowledge and understanding of each unit or topic. Is there a part of the syllabus that you have not taught before? Was last year's work covered in full? How will you link this part of the syllabus to last year's work, earlier lessons or to other topics?

Plan ahead:

- Read the textbook and teacher's manual carefully – they may be your only resource.

Activity *Making notes*

- **Size and arrangement**

How many pupils are in the class? How can groups be organised? Is it possible to change the organisation for some lessons?

- **Age and ability**

Are the lesson content and activities set at the right level?

- **Learning needs**

Not all pupils learn in the same way. Have you provided a range of learning opportunities?

- **Motivation**

Learning achievement is very closely linked to pupil interest. How do you gain interest from the very start of the lesson?

- **Behaviour**

What are the rules and routines that must be understood? Are there any pupils with behaviour problems? How are these dealt with in your school?

- **Previous work with this subject**

What do the pupils know already? How will this part of the syllabus be linked to last year's work, earlier lessons or to other topics?

- Find time to visit a local teachers' resource centre for any reference books. If there is a museum in your area you may also find information there.
- Get together with other teachers in your school or find out if there is a cluster meeting where you can meet other teachers and share ideas about teaching this part of the syllabus.
- Keep notes about your findings.

(See Knowledge, Topic 1)

Organisation and management

Find out as much as you can about the class that you are going to teach. This is particularly important for a student/trainee or newly qualified teacher. It is equally important for more experienced staff each time they teach a new group of pupils. (See also the whole of Section 2, Organisation.)

Available resources

Be thoroughly familiar with the teaching and learning resources available for your class. If you plan ahead you will have time to make new resources, organise a field trip, or make use of knowledgeable parents or other members of the community.

- Are there sufficient textbooks for all pupils?
- Are there books for all the subjects to be taught?
- Is there a teacher's manual available for you or can you borrow one from the head or another teacher?
- What teaching aids are available?
- Is there a resource room or library in the school?
- Is there a nearby Teachers' Resource Centre?
- What teaching aids will you need to collect or make?
- If resources are shared, is there a place where the items are stored? Is there a clear arrangement so that you can have the materials when you need them?

Methods and strategies

No teaching method is clearly the best. Some teachers follow a traditional approach. They prefer to make decisions about learning. Others may prefer a more flexible approach and allow pupils to make some decisions about their learning programme. The best teachers are those that are able to use a variety of methods and activities. If you have used the same method for several terms, try using a new teaching method at least once a term. (See Topic 39 Choosing the best method and Topic 25 Making learning active.)

Assessment

Finally, spend some time planning how you will make assessments of both your lessons and the learning of your pupils. Prepare observation sheets, pupil files, Record of Marks sheets, etc. They will help you fill in your continuous assessment forms and report sheets more accurately and save hours of work later in the term.

17 Schemes of work

Activity Look ahead

In the chart below

- Divide the Maths syllabus into units of work.
- Sub-divide each unit into essential topics that **must** be covered and optional topics that could be postponed until later.
- Gradually fill in the columns during the term.

Your Ministry of Education has probably developed national guidelines that outline the topics to be covered in each subject included in the primary curriculum. The ministry will also indicate the number of lessons to be taught in each subject and the length of time for each lesson. This information provides the basis for the Schemes of Work that teachers make showing how they intend to cover the syllabus during the coming year. Ideally, they should be planned with the head and year-group teachers at the end of the year and reviewed or modified at the end of each term. Properly prepared, a detailed scheme of work can:

- identify what has been covered during the each term and what had to be left out. A teacher is then in a better position to make realistic changes for the following year.
- help year-group teachers ensure that each class covers the same amount of work by keeping track of topics taught in each class.
- give teachers who take the class during the next year a clearer idea of what areas have been covered.

This chart shows how your scheme might look for three of the Mathematics Units to be taught in Term 1. It can be adapted for each subject in the syllabus.

Scheme of Work – Term Plan						
Subject Mathematics		**Class 4** **Name of Teacher**		**Term 1:** **Units to be covered: 6** **e.g. 1 Number, 2 Fractions, 3 Time, 4 Area** **5 Shape, 6 Measurement**		
	Essential Topics	**Completed**	**Reason not completed**	**Optional Topics**	**Date completed**	**Omitted**
Unit 1 Number **Number of Topics 4**	*e.g.* *Add/subtract (3 digits)* *Multiplication tables (8 and 9)* *Multiply (2 digits)* *Prime numbers and multiples*	*Week 1 & 2* *Week 4* *Week 5 & 6* *Week 7*		*Doubling and Halving* *Square numbers* *Tables and graphs (whole numbers)*	*Week 4* *Week 4*	*To do later*
Unit 2 *Fractions* **Number of Topics 3**	**e.g.** *equivalent fractions* *Mixed numbers* *Top-heavy fractions*	*Week 3* *Week 7 & 8*		*Simple calculations* *adding/subtracting* *Multiplying*	*Week 8*	*To do later*
Unit 3 *Time* **Number of Topics 2**	*24 hour clock* *Time tables*	*Week 8 unfinished* *Week 9*	*Rain for three days*	*Calculations involving time*		*To do later*

Units of Work

The chart below details the scheme of work for one of the Maths units to be taught in Term 1 in more detail showing:

1 The content of the main topic areas.
2 Likely problem areas
3 The way the topic can be linked to previous and future topics

The main problems with completing the syllabus.

- **Loss of teaching time** The school or certain classes may be involved in rehearsals for regional or national events. There may also be a number of days lost due to heavy rain or periods of drought.
- **Insufficient teaching hours** Where schools have to run a double or triple shift system.
- **An overloaded curriculum** The amount of time allocated to each subject may be insufficient for the number of topics included in the syllabus.
- **Staff shortages**

Many teachers work steadily through the syllabus only to find that some important topics have not been covered. Be realistic, work with the head and other teachers in your year group to design a flexible Scheme of Work.

Scheme of Work – Mathematics
Class 4 Term 1:
Unit 1 – Number Work

Number of Essential Topics in the Number Unit 4 Add/subtract (3 digits numbers) Week 1 & 2 Multiplication tables (8 and 9) Week 4 Multiply (2 digit numbers) Week 5 and 6 Prime numbers and multiple Week 7 **Number of Optional Topics in the Number Unit 3** Doubling and Halving Square numbers Tables and graphs (whole numbers)	
Problem areas that need special teaching aids	e.g. Make 10 × 10 grids for multiplication tables prime numbers and square numbers Make a 24 hour clock face for Unit on time
extra information	Find more information on Time Zones and the International Date Line
Links with previous topics	e.g. Prime numbers can be linked with earlier work on odd and even numbers
Links with future topics	e.g. Prime numbers and Multiples will link with Highest Common Factors and Lowest Common Multiples Graphs can be linked to science topics 24 hour clock to time zones

18 Lesson plans

Include some of these in your plan

- Aims and objectives
- Content (subject matter)
- Resources and teaching aids
- The teaching method or approach
- Learning activities or tasks
- An evaluation of the lesson
- Organisation of the class
- Timing for each section
- Alternate activities
- Problem areas
- Homework

All teachers, both those who are newly qualified and those who are more experienced, need to plan their lessons well in advance. Your school may require you to prepare lesson plans either on a weekly or a daily basis. The list in the margin shows some of the sections that may have to be included. Are there any other details that you should have in your lesson plans?

Aims and objectives

Stating clear aims and objectives for a lesson allows you to organise the learning outcomes properly and should be clearly linked to previous and future learning. It is useful to ask yourself these questions:

- What information do I expect my pupils to learn during this lesson?
- What skills will they use or need to learn?
- How does this lesson relate to previous learning?
- How will this lesson be linked to future topics?

Content

Your knowledge and understanding of a subject will affect the way that you teach. If this is a subject or topic area in which you feel less than confident try to get help from other teachers or from a resource centre. Not all lessons will have the same content. Your lesson should always start from 'the existing knowledge of the class', their knowledge of the topic and their skills, and this may vary from year to year. (See Knowledge Topic 1.)

Be prepared

- Read the textbook and teacher's subject manual carefully.
- Decide how much information you need to give. How will you explain the topic? Try to find a way to make the lesson interesting and stimulating to pupils and remember to relate the learning to the experience of your pupils. (See Teaching skills, Topic 3.)
- Think ahead. What might prove difficult? How will you deal with questions and difficulties?

Resources and teaching aids

What resources will you need to use during the lesson? There may be some already available, others may need preparation.

Activity *Making use of all your resources*

Look at a number of the lesson plans you have prepared this term. Do they make use of more than one of the following resources?

- The ideas and experiences of your pupils.
- Activity or work cards.
- The chalkboard.
- Pictures or objects to illustrate the lesson.
- Activities that will allow pupils to be creative.

Which of these resources do you need to make more use of?

Teaching methods

The section on teaching methods (Choosing the best method, Topic 39) gives more information on various choices that you can make. Sometimes you will want to focus your pupils' attention on some information that you want them to learn. Avoid using teacher-centred methods for too much of the lesson. Your pupils will learn more effectively if you use child-centred methods that focus attention on the contribution that they can make to the lesson. You will also find that they will respond better to a variety of different methods.

Activities

The variety of activities that can be carried out will depend on the age and ability of the class. (See Making learning active, Topic 25.) Some lessons work well with groups, others are better if pupils work by themselves. Make sure that tasks suit the needs of the full range of pupils. Prepare a few more difficult activities for those who work quickly and some easier exercises for those with learning difficulties. Do not rely on note-taking. Encourage the class to think for themselves.

Monitoring and evaluation

It is important to build an evaluation of your lesson into your lesson plans. (See Evaluating your performance, Topic 8.) Pupil monitoring and assessment should be on-going during the lesson.
It may be carried out through observation, questions and activities. You need to evaluate how far you have succeeded in achieving the aims and objectives of your lesson.

Not all planning takes place before the lesson

It is sometimes necessary to modify the plan during the lesson. You need to be flexible.

- Think about the existing knowledge of pupils. They may know more than you first thought.
- Be aware of unanticipated learning needs. The pupils may not have understood an earlier lesson and so you will have to spend extra time going over this work.
- Remember there may be interruptions. A pupil may be taken ill, or resources may not be available.

Activity *Assessment and monitoring*

What assessment techniques do you use during your lesson?

- How would you monitor individual learning progress?
- How would you monitor group learning?
- How would you monitor the strength or weakness of your lesson?

Activity *Plan a lesson in one area of the syllabus*

You can use your ministry lesson plan to do this.

- Identify two or three objectives you would like to attain during the lesson. (See Aims and objectives opposite.)
- Identify at least two different resources you will use.
- What methods will you use to teach the beginning of the lesson to involve pupils?
- What methods of assessment will you use to make sure that individuals and groups achieve the objectives of your lesson?
- Evaluate your plan with another teacher.

19 Lesson presentation skills

Presentation skills

- **Setting the scene**: beginning the lesson.
- **Clarity**: voice, explanations, instructions.
- **Monitoring**.
- **Ending the lesson:** summarising the learning.
- **Timing**: moving from one part of the lesson to another, or from whole class to group or individual activities.

Activity

Introducing Topics

Choose a lesson that you will teach during the next week and plan the opening of that lesson using each of these methods.

1 Use two or three pictures illustrating the topic and tell pupils about them.
2 Start with a story linked to the topic.
3 Ask groups to collect information about the topic before the lesson.

Teaching is very like acting. A good play gets your interest right from the start and a good performance stays in your memory for a long time. Think about your performance in your lessons in the same way.

Setting the scene

Always be punctual and ready to start your lessons. The first five minutes are very important and need careful planning. Have books and resource materials ready and prepare experiments or group work before your pupils arrive.

Introducing the topic

- Gain everyone's attention and interest immediately, by saying and/or doing something that will focus attention on the lesson.
- Provide a framework for the lesson saying what it is about. Pupils learn best when they understand what is expected of them. For example, say, **Today we are going to .... and you are going to learn about/how to .....**
- Move from the known to the unknown. Link the lesson to something that pupils already know. A short question and answer session will help them to remember what they know already. This can be linked to the new material.

Clarity

Make sure that your lessons have a clear plan.

- Make your instructions clear before activities begin.
- Give a clear explanation of the content of the lesson.
- Make sure work written on the board is easy to read and understand.

Monitoring

Don't stay behind your desk all the time. You will find out far more about the learning needs of your pupils by moving around the class as they work on activities.

Ending the lesson

The last few minutes of the lesson are as important as the first. Group and individual activities should have been completed. You should be the focus of attention. (See Whole class teaching, Topic 32.)

Evaluating work

- Get feedback from activities and check that everyone has understood the lesson.
- Summarise the key points and try to ask a number of questions that will really test your pupil's understanding.
- Reinforce links with earlier lessons. Refer to the way this lesson will link with the next.: **Next lesson we will .....**
- Give a short quiz.
- Homework should be used to reinforce or extend the learning of this lesson or prepare for the next. Do not overuse homework as an excuse to make up for lost time, e.g. **You can finish this off for homework**.

In the last few moments:

- Make sure everyone has finished the work from the chalkboard.
- Have pupils written down homework activities clearly?
- Make a note of unfinished work or of any points that need to be followed up during later lessons.

Timing

Even if the topic is interesting, a lesson plan will fail if the timing is neglected. There is very little time in 35 to 40 minutes to attend to the needs of different groups or the special needs of individuals. It is very easy to over-run.

The chart will help you to work out your timing of the lesson.

This chart will help you to work out the timing of your lessons

Total time:	35 minutes	**Points to remember**
Settling the class **Introduction** 'setting the scene'	1 to 2 minutes 2 to 3 minutes	Make a timetable and keep to it. Pace relates to the way that a lesson moves. All sections of the lesson should be timed.
Main content Finding prior knowledge Explanation and questions Instructions relating to activities	**10 to 12 minutes** (1 to 2 minutes) 7 minutes 2 to 3 minutes	Know how long each section of the lesson will take and understand how to vary the pace of the lesson.
Learning activities Activity 1 Activity 2 Activity 3	**15 minutes** 5 minutes 5 minutes 5 minutes	Some sections will need to be done slowly and carefully to make sure that everyone understands, e.g. the demonstration of long multiplication. Others can make use of speed, e.g. a mental arithmetic test.
Monitoring	During activity time	This has to take into account checking group work and helping individuals.
Closing Session Summary of learning Testing knowledge Clearing up	4 to 5 minutes	

20 Planning outside visits

Excursions outside the school should be an important part of the learning experience of all primary school pupils. They may include field trips, visits to local places of interest, or to other schools for sports, drama or music programmes. Visits need to be planned carefully.

- What is the purpose of the visit and what do you hope to achieve?
- How will you organise the visit?

How can your local area be used in teaching?

The cost of transport often makes it impossible to make long trips with students. There will, however, be places of interest in your local area that can be used to illustrate topics in the curriculum. Most pupils walk to school every day but they may not notice features of interest such as a small stream, crops growing on farms or interesting local buildings. Children in towns and cities may go to market, travel on a bus or visit a hospital without linking what they experience with learning activities.

Planning your visit

- Plan visits as a way of introducing a topic or as a practical activity linked to class work that has already been introduced. Always try to take advantage of any special events in your local area. If possible, go to the place yourself, before taking your pupils. Then you will be able to show them things of interest and tell them what they need to know. They can use the information in a project or exercise later.
- Use one lesson to link the visit to lessons and explain what you want your pupils to look for.
- Let individual pupils and groups know what information they will need to collect and what tasks they will need to complete after the visit. You can decide to give pupils a general work sheet with a variety of things to do or questions to answer. Or you can divide the class into smaller groups, and give each group a particular task. (See Using the local area, Topic 58.) Information, worksheets and/or assignments will have to be prepared before the visit. Encourage your pupils to prepare some of this material themselves.
- During the visit, and again before returning to the school, make sure that each group has the information it needs to complete the assignments.
- After the visit, when you return to school, go over the important points and make sure that everyone is quite clear about their assignment and how it will be done.

Activity *Using your local area*

Make a list of places of interest in your local area that could be included in a visit outside the school.

How can visits be used in different areas of the curriculum?

Safety issues

There may be regulations concerning the number of children each teacher should supervise. In some circumstances there should be one teacher for every 20 pupils. This is an area where parents might be asked to help. (See Involving parents in school activities, Topic 68.) Each adult should have a checklist of the pupils in his/her care.

- Make sure that every pupil knows the rules of road safety before you go out.
- Before visiting any place of work with the pupils, visit it yourself so that you can warn them of any hazards.
- Discuss safety with the pupils. Get them to compile a list of common sense rules, e.g. do not leave the group without telling someone where you are going; do not pick anything up without asking permission. Keep a list of these rules where the pupils can see them. They can be updated at any time. (See Developing discussion, Topic 27.) Other examples of common sense rules: Keep together;

  Behave sensibly at all times;

  Respect other adults/helpers;

  Look out for each other.
- If the excursion is in a town, near a busy road, or to some other area such as a river that could be dangerous, you will need to give very detailed instructions about the way pupils should walk and behave and appoint responsible group leaders from the class who can help you keep everyone together.

- If the pupils have been working with local people, or asking them questions, suggest that they write a letter of thanks.

Organisation of the visit

If you have not taken your class on an excursion before, begin with a visit to a place that is in or very near your school compound.

People to inform

Always discuss proposed visits with the head of school first. The head should have information concerning guidelines laid down by the local education authority. You or the head may legally be required to inform the local education officer. Parents should also be told about intended visits, especially if the pupils are going any distance from the school.

A simple form like the one below can be sent to each parent.

Taboro Primary School

Dear Parent,

As part of our study of the local area, pupils in Class 3 will study the buildings along the Taboro Road between 10.00 a.m. and 12.00 noon on Friday October 16th.

Each pupil will have individual and group work to complete. Please make sure that your child has his/her notebook and pencil on that day. Their work will be displayed later in the term on Open Day.

If any parent would like to help with this excursion, particularly by taking charge of a group of pupils, please let either the head or the class teacher know by Monday of next week.

Yours sincerely

Miss Kabo

21 Time management

Teachers have to carry out a great variety of tasks. These include administrative duties, planning activities, classroom organisation, the preparation of teaching aids, marking, detailed record-keeping and meetings with colleagues, parents and pupils. They also need to be able to find time for their own personal and professional development. This section will help you to improve the management of your personal time and the management of lesson time.

Personal time management

To be able to manage your time successfully you will need to find out exactly how much time you spend on different activities during your school day. At first you may think this is just another time-consuming activity, but the findings will help you to make better use of your day.

The suggested time sheet is one example of the way you can do this. You may think of other ways.

Activity *A suggested time sheet*

Keep a record of the tasks you regularly do over a week.

Start Date	**Time**	**Comment**	**End Date**	**Time**	**Comment**
Teaching tasks					
Lesson planning and preparation			Locating/preparing teaching aids		
Explanation of lesson			Pupil activities		
Marking			Others		
Administrative Tasks					
Registration			Organising room or resources		
Writing reports			Entering records		
Playground or			Other		
Boarding house duties					
Non teaching duties					
Staff meetings			Interviews with parents		
Out-of school activities/clubs, sports etc.			In-service activities or programmes		
Other Tasks					

Managing your time more effectively

Think about the tasks you have to carry out

Some tasks need to be carried out weekly or even daily. Others can be planned well ahead of time. Reports, for example, may need to be completed each term. Make sure that you are keeping up-to-date records of all the information you will need. Fill in the administrative details early in the term and keep an observation sheet of the attitudes and progress of each pupil as the term proceeds. (See Keeping records, Topic 65.) If there are regular examinations, you may find it useful to make a note of possible examination questions for each subject as topics are completed.

What are your priorities?

Take a good look at the duties and tasks you have to do. Decide which ones are the most important and work out ways to make better use of your time in school.

Make a list of tasks you **must** do:

- Every day.
- At the end of each week.
- At the end of each term.
- At the end of each year.

Learn to delegate or share tasks

It may not be appropriate to delegate or share tasks all the time. Many teachers, however, regularly delegate routine tasks to pupils. You will save a lot of time if you prepare some lessons or teaching aids with another teacher. (See Working with other staff, Topic 67.)

Management of lesson time

Time management of lessons is an important skill. Do not be too ambitious. If you try to cover too much you will not be able to finish all the work planned. It is very easy to find that you have spent too long on explanations and that you have left too little time for activities or responses from pupils. (See Lesson presentation skills, Topic 19.) Learn how to plan the timing of your lessons.

Activities that can slow a lesson down

1 Reading aloud by someone who is not very confident of their skill

- Give pupils some writing and listen to individuals read.
- Pair pupils. (See Pair work, Topic 34.)
- Add variety by allowing pupils to read from supplementary reading books or a newspaper.

Monitor these activities by listening to the level of noise in the class. (See Managing large classes, Topic 18.)

2 Too many examples (e.g. sums) being done by individual pupils on the board

This may interest good students, but many will pay no attention.

- Allow a few examples on the board and then break the class into smaller groups with a leader.
- Pair pupils. (See Pair work, Topic 34.)

Long note writing

Where there are few textbooks some teachers write detailed notes on the board. This does not encourage thinking.

- Write **ONLY** the important points or key words on the board.

Encourage pupils to find their own words. (See Using the chalkboard, Topic 54.)

22 Homework

Giving your pupils a little homework each week helps to reinforce their learning. In many homes, however, it is difficult for pupils to find the time or a place to do these assignments.

Parents may not understand the way that homework can improve the progress of their children. They may expect them to do chores or look after younger brothers and sisters when they return from school. Even when they understand its importance there may be nowhere for the child to do the homework. Schools, particularly those working on a single shift, can help by allowing pupils to do their homework in class immediately after school.

What kind of homework should be given?

As far as possible, use homework exercises to follow up the last lesson or prepare for the next. For example, some homework could be given after one of the lessons in Topic 56, Making the best use of limited resources. Pupils could find three or four words they do not know the meaning of in the newspaper and use each word in a new sentence, or write a short paragraph about a country mentioned in the news. They might be asked to learn words for spelling and to make four sentences of their own from the spelling words.

How much homework should you give?

You need to plan your homework timetable and the exercises you give very carefully. Because of the home situation of many of your pupils you will be aware that very few of them will be able to do more than half an hour's homework each day. Plan to give short exercises that pupils can do quickly by themselves. These can be marked or tested easily either by you or by the pupils.

You may decide to give homework in the basic subjects only. You could ask the pupils to do two homework assignments each week in English and Mathematics and one in Science or Social/Environment Studies (five assignments in all). You should try to vary the kind of exercise that you give. Be realistic! You will not have time to mark a lot of written work. Ask pupils to learn something by heart, e.g. a rhyme or spelling words, or give an exercise that asks pupils to find out information for the next lesson. Both of these types of exercise can be tested orally. Pupils do not need to sit down and write formally, though they may make notes. Occasionally you can give them some written work.

How can parents help?

Explain to the parents, perhaps at a PTA meeting, how important it is to support their children's homework and to provide a clean place where they can sit and work.

- Encourage parents to provide a table and stool and some sort of light if homework has to be done in the evening.
- Encourage parents to ask what homework has to be done that day and to make sure that it is completed properly and returned to school the next day.
- Display a copy of the timetable in your classroom or create a special page in an exercise book so that they know what subject is covered each day and what exercise has to be done.
- Stress that homework is to reinforce learning. It is not helpful if the child is given too much help either by the parent an older brother or sister or an afternoon teacher.

Activity *Creating a homework timetable based on the subjects taught each day during the week*

	Monday	Tuesday	Wednesday	Thursday	Friday
Subject					

A homework routine

- At the end of your lesson write the homework clearly on the board and make sure pupils have understood what they have to do and have copied the instructions into their notebooks.
- Appoint a class monitor or group leaders to collect any written homework the next morning, immediately after registration.
- Make sure that you go over the homework as soon as possible.
  1. Give a short quiz to test spelling.
  2. Ask pupils to recite, e.g. a poem (individually or in a small group).
  3. Question pupils about information you may have asked them to find out when you introduce the next lesson.
- When you mark written homework make a note of individual problems. (See Keeping records, Topic 65.) Try to give those pupils help as you monitor the class during the next lesson.
- Evaluate the success of your lesson through the answers given in the homework. If some errors occur frequently it may be because you did not teach that section of the lesson sufficiently clearly. You may need to go over it again in another way. (See Evaluating your performance, Topic 8.)

23 Questioning skills

> ***Activity*** *Question categories*
>
> Make a list of some of the types of question you might ask during your lesson.
>
> • These questions can be quite simple and related to lesson management:
>
> Have you all handed in your homework?
>
> Has everyone found the correct page?
>
> • They can ask for the application or recall of previously learned knowledge:
>
> How many times will 5 divide into 25?
>
> • They can help pupils build on what they already know or solve a problem:
>
> What are the differences between a market and a shop?
>
> If we did not have clocks and watches how could we tell the time?

The best way to involve pupils in the learning process is through questions. Studies in different countries have found that most teachers ask between 300 and 400 questions a day. In a typical lesson, you may use questions to create interest in the topic, find out what pupils already know, stimulate thinking or to find out how far they have understood the lesson.

Identifying different types of question

Closed questions are used most frequently. They require only a 'Yes' or 'No' answer, or are questions with only one answer, e.g. What is the name of the largest lake in Africa?
By asking a closed question you can find out:

- If a pupil remembers what he/she learned today, yesterday or during the last lesson.
- If he/she has understood the lesson.
- If he/she knows enough to be able solve similar problems.

To help pupils develop thinking skills every lesson should contain more open-ended questions. An open-ended question has many possible answers. These questions allow pupils to guess, give an opinion, a reason or an explanation from the facts they already know. It is important that pupils are encouraged to express their own ideas.

- **What will happen if ....?**
- **Why does this happen ....?**
- **How can we explain ....?**

What will happen to our village if there is no rain for many years?

Why should we wash fruit and vegetables bought in the market?

Using questions effectively

As you prepare your lesson plan give some thought to the questions you want to ask and how you are going to ask them. You will get the best results if you think of a variety of **key questions** and prepare them as part of the lesson plan.

- Your questions will then be clear and relevant to the topic.
- They can be linked together, gradually building up learning during the lesson.

Prepared questions can be asked with particular pupils in mind: more difficult questions for bright students; easier questions to increase the confidence of slow or timid students.

Helpful hints

1. Start from what pupils already know.
2. Use a variety of questions and be ready to ask a question in another way if the pupil has difficulty giving an answer.
3. Use simple words that are easily understood.
4. Give everyone a chance to answer questions at some time during each day.
5. Do not allow pupils to shout out the answer. Encourage them to put up their hands.
6. Listen carefully to pupils' answers (they may lead on to other questions that will help build up knowledge).
7. Be ready to admit when you do not know an answer yourself. Suggest how the class could find out. (This could be a task for one of the brighter groups.)

Avoid questions that invite a straight 'yes ' or 'no' answer.
Encourage pupils to solve problems and to THINK.

Who do you ask?

The whole class

At the beginning of the lesson it is often useful to ask a number of quick questions that will involve the whole class. These may link the new lesson to what has been learned previously. They can provide an opportunity for you to find out what the pupils already know about the new topic.

- Don't ask only the bright pupils and ignore the rest – give every pupil a chance to answer.
- Make sure that you ask the girls as well as the boys.

Small groups or individuals

As the topic develops small groups or individuals can be given more difficult open-ended questions to answer as part of the activities.

Getting a response to questions

You need to get as many of the class as possible to contribute to the lesson.
Then you can make use of pupils' answers to develop learning.

Try different strategies to involve everyone.

- **Pause** after asking a question to allow pupils' time to think.
- **Prompt** slow learners by asking the question in a different way if a pupil does not seem to have understood the first time.
- **Encourage** shy pupils or those with learning difficulties by praising their answers.
- **Stretch** brighter pupils by asking more difficult questions.
- **Avoid** using scorn and ridicule if the answer is incorrect.
- **Praise** correct answers and encourage pupils to develop their answers further.

24 Giving explanations

Activity *Using explanations*

Teachers use explanations in many different ways.

- They can describe the purpose or topic of the lesson.
- They can give instructions about activities.
- They can be used to answer questions.

Teachers also use explanations to help the pupils understand:

- Consequences: If we do this then this will happen.
- New ideas: Such as conservation or citizenship.
- Reasons: Plants need air and light to grow because .....
- Processes: The correct way to multiply or divide decimal fractions.
- Relationships: The way climate affects natural vegetation.

List the different ways you use explanations in your class.

One of the most important teaching skills is the ability to give clear explanations. What are we trying to do when we give explanations in class? A dictionary would define the activity as **helping with understanding.**

Effective explanations

Explaining is not the same as lecturing. It should be a two-way process and take into account the knowledge of the listeners and the questions they may want to ask.

Before giving an explanation

Find out what pupils already know. You may be surprised at the amount of knowledge that they have already learned from radio, films, TV, newspapers or books and by talking to others. You may also find that some of that knowledge is not correct.

The way that you use your voice can make a lot of difference. Think about talks or lectures you have listened to at college or on the radio. A good speaker will vary the level of his/her voice, emphasise certain words with gestures, change the pace and use pauses or will add something to make the audience laugh. Each of these strategies is designed to keep listeners interested. If pupils are interested in a topic they are more likely to remember what the lesson was about.

Giving an explanation

1 Make sure that the language you use is simple and clear.

2 Be clear about the way that you will give the explanation.

- Try to relate the explanation to the experience of the listeners.
- Identify the main points and highlight these on the board.
- Arrange your information in order and link important points together.
- Use a number of similar examples to illustrate the idea you are explaining.
- Give plenty of opportunity for pupils to contribute.
- Use teaching aids and activities that will reinforce or extend understanding.

This outline does not mean that all your explanations should follow the same pattern. There are different ways in which a new topic can be explained.

Activity Beginning a new topic

Make a note of the way you begin explaining a new topic.

Do you:

- Immediately start with a lot of facts and information?
- Ask a pupil to read the information from the textbook?
- Write the heading on the board and then ask, 'Who can tell me something about?'
- Begin by telling a short story or giving an interesting piece of information that will lead into an explanation of the topic?

Activity Different approaches

Choose a topic that you know well and try out each approach described above to plan your opening.

- Make pupils guess what you are going to talk about.
- Find out what pupils already know.
- Briefly outline what they are going to learn about.

Try each approach in class and see which gets the best result.

This may be an opportunity to work with another teacher, who will also be teaching the topic.

How far have your pupils understood your explanations?

If pupils are to develop their level of understanding they need to be able to answer questions properly and give clear explanations both to you and to each other.

Improving pupil explanations

Answering questions

Usually the first response that pupils give to a question is very brief. It may not give you a clear idea about their level of understanding. Use more probing questions to get more detail. (See Questioning skills, Topic 23.)

Instead of explaining an activity to the whole class try telling one member of each group. Let him/her explain what needs to be done to the rest of the group. Even though groups usually have a leader it is a good idea to give this opportunity to other members. Then each one has a chance to develop his/her communication skills.

Explaining unfamiliar topics

At some time every teacher is asked to explain something that they are not familiar with or that they do not fully understand themselves. This is more likely to happen in subjects like Science in upper primary classes but even very young pupils can ask awkward questions.

Possible actions

- Admit that you do not know.
- Avoid answering the question or teaching difficult topics.
- See if anyone in the class can answer the question.
- Encourage pupils to look for the answer in reference books or a library (where these are available).

The first of these options is better than the second because it is honest. If you admit to a lack of knowledge you can encourage pupils to find out the information for themselves. If you deal with the problem positively you are unlikely to lose the respect of your pupils.

A lack of knowledge and understanding of certain topics will affect your teaching and the learning achievement of your pupils. If these are topics that have to be taught you will need to take further action yourself.

Getting help

- reference books
- a subject co-ordinator
- a Teachers' Resource Centre (if there is one nearby)
- from another teacher *or*
- a more knowledgeable friend.

25 Making learning active

Topic 4, The process of learning, describes different ways of learning. Some pupils prefer working on their own; others like group activities. Some prefer reading books; others enjoy practical activities. Textbooks provide exercises designed to reinforce the learning but these tend to follow a similar pattern. They may not provide as much variety as you might like.

What is active learning?

Active learning is learning by doing. It includes role-play, project work, investigation and problem solving. This approach to learning requires preparation as the teacher needs to develop a variety of activities. However, it is worthwhile in the long run because it gradually develops greater levels of skill and understanding and also improves pupil motivation and attitudes to learning.

How can you make your lessons more active?

Topic 27, Developing discussion gives an example of **brainstorming** and shows how you can get ideas from your pupils.

- Write **TRANSPORT** in large letters in the centre of the board then very quickly ask each pupil to give you **one** word connected with transport. Write their ideas around the word.
- Let one group of pupils develop a short drama or role-play: **Who am I?** They can act as someone selling goods to people in cars as they wait in traffic, or as a driver at the local lorry station. Each 'role-play' would require that the group uses the right vocabulary and acts the part well enough for others to guess who they are.
- Use alphabet and word games to extend vocabulary as individual, team or group activities. Find a word beginning with each of the letters of the alphabet. Use a theme such as Roads or Travel: a = accident; b = bypass; c = car; d = detour; e = emergency, and so on.
- Ask your pupils to prepare a questionnaire for a traffic survey: **Why do people use transport?** (See Planning outside visits, Topic 20.) Your pupils could also use their questionnaires for topics on the local environment.

Example

Imagine you are teaching about transport. How can you make your pupils really think about the topic?

Activity *Active learning*

Choose a topic in your Environment Studies textbook. Make a list of the important ideas that you want your pupils to learn about.

What part of the topic could be used in a short drama or role-play?

What new words could be mimed?

What game could you play that would develop new words related to the topic?

Activity *Active learning in Maths*

Here is a list of topics you might have to teach:

Fractions, Weights and measures, Co-ordinates, Graphs, Measuring Area and Perimeter.

Which of the following ideas could you use to make these topics more interesting?

- A menu for a party.
- A treasure hunt in the school compound.
- Cars passing along the road in front to the school.
- The height of your pupils or the size of their feet.

Active learning in English

Getting pupils to think about ideas for story writing can be an active way of helping them learn to write compositions.

- Invent a story

This activity is more effective with groups of six or eight pupils.

The first person in the group makes up a sentence to start the story: *'The farmer looked up at the sky....'*

Each person in the group then adds one sentence to continue the story. The sentence given by the last person has to end the story.

Get one or two pupils in each group to write down the sentences. The stories can be shared with other groups or displayed.

Active learning in Maths

Maths can be very dull if it is just a series of sums to complete. What kinds of activities are particularly suited to Maths lessons?

Active learning in Science

Science topics provide many opportunities for active learning.

- Asking questions.
- Observing.
- Experimenting.
- Making accurate recordings.
- Identifying, classifying, sorting and sequencing.

Learning can be made more active in one lesson in a lower primary Science class by, for example, getting pupils to experiment by using their senses.

Example: Five senses

Instead of explaining the five senses to the children verbally, begin the lesson by asking them to complete a series of group activities. These will enable them to understand how they use their sense of: **seeing**, **hearing**, **tasting**, **touching** and **smelling**.

You will need a blindfold and a number of objects hidden in a box (one for each group). These might include an orange or an onion, some salt or sugar crystals, a piece of wood or leather, some rice or beans, an article of clothing, a sponge or any suitable objects that may be available. Choose some unusual items that are not too easy to guess so that the pupils have to use the different senses.

After they have finished the activity ask pupils questions about the senses that they used to identify the objects.

- If you cannot see, which senses help you identify where you are and what is around you?
- If you have no sense of smell can you still tell the difference between the taste of salt and sugar, or an orange and an onion?

26 Children talking to each other

> ### *Activity* *Hearing what children say*
>
> Try to spend time listening to what pupils are talking about. What are their conversations usually about?
>
> - Borrowing something, e.g. a book, a pencil, an eraser, a ruler?
> - Asking another pupil how to do the activity or exercise?
> - Talking about the work in hand – sharing ideas?
> - Talking about something unrelated to the lesson?

One of the most difficult decisions you have to make is whether to allow pupils to talk to each other during lessons. Should talking be regarded as part of the learning process or is it just time-wasting?

Learning through talk

Children in Africa usually have to develop skills in more than one language. In their early primary years, they may be taught in a local language that may or may not be their mother tongue. (See Language policy, Topic 5.) Later on, classes use English as the language of instruction. Fluency in any language can only be developed where pupils are given opportunities to express themselves and develop their own ideas.

Should children be seen and not heard?

In the past a good class was thought to be one where the teacher gave instructions and the pupils then worked silently on written tasks. Today we believe that social skills and learning achievement in all subjects are actually improved when pupils have an opportunity to **question**, **discuss**, **describe**, **explain** and **argue**.

There will always be a certain amount of general chatting in a classroom. As a teacher you should try to encourage pupils to share ideas even though this may lead to slightly higher levels of noise in your class.

Developing speaking skills

In every lesson teachers ask questions, but these can often be answered very briefly. Try to ask more open-ended questions (see Questioning skills, Topic 23) to provide pupils with opportunities to develop their skills in speaking and listening. Try also to give each pupil more time to talk. This may not always be possible during

whole class teaching, especially in large classes, but it is possible during pairwork or group activities.

Provide opportunities for children to develop talking skills

Asking questions

Pupils often recite, **How are you?** and get the reply, **I am very well thank you.** This kind of recitation may prevent the development of conversation because a ready-made answer has been provided.

- Ask pairs of pupils to develop their own questions. They can test them on each other and then on other pairs. Make sure that questions cannot be answered by 'yes' or 'no' or by a single word and that pupils gradually learn to ask open-ended questions. (See Questioning skills, Topic 23.)
- Encourage them to probe by asking other related questions.
- Each group can make flashcards that ask a variety of simple questions. These can be exchanged among the groups. Listen to pupils asking these questions and make corrections as you move around the groups.

You will probably find that most children enjoy talking but are less keen to listen to someone else. You should also use talking skills to encourage listening skills.

Are your pupils given an opportunity to:

- Ask each other questions?
- Give instructions that others must follow?
- Describe real events that they have observed?
- Debate/discuss real issues?

Example

1. What did you do during the holiday?
2. Which story did you like best this term?
3. What was the story about?
4. Which character did you like best?

Giving instructions

- Working in pairs, one pupil gives instructions for a simple task. The partner must carry out the instructions exactly. This will also teach pupils how to sequence instructions accurately (**first**, **next** or **then**).

Sequencing

This is how you should put on a shirt or a pair of shoes:

This is how you draw a simple shape:

First you...

Next you ...

Then you ...

News items

- A local football match.
- Walking home from school.
- Children's own news.

Discussion and debate

Traditionally younger children find it difficult to disagree with the views of their parents, teacher or even older brothers and sisters. It is important to get pupils to express their own ideas and to think about the ideas and opinions of others.

Use a discussion about real issues (in a Health and Safety lesson for example) to encourage pupils to pick out the important ideas and to ask questions that will help them understand new ideas. Let them express their own opinions.

Differences of opinion can lead to quarrels. Your role is to act as a mediator. You need to help them understand that people do not always have to agree.

27 Developing discussion

Discussions between both teacher and pupil, and between pairs or small groups of pupils, often develop from questions that have been asked. They are an important part of the learning process. They provide a chance to make points clearly, express an opinion and listen to what others have to say. (See Children talking to each other, Topic 26 which looks at different ways that discussion can be developed within small groups of pupils.) This section will look more specifically at teacher-directed discussion.

***Activity** Organising the topic into themes*

Help pupils identify the main themes from their ideas.

- The weather and its effect on roads.
- People who use the roads.
- Safety issues.
- Road building and maintenance.

Organising a discussion

Sometimes discussion develops quite naturally out of the lesson. Many textbooks look at environment or community issues. A news item might be about a forest fire or an oil spillage in the sea. Within the local community there will also be issues that are important, e.g. the shortage of water in homes or the state of the roads. There is scope for a lot of discussion practice in pairs or in groups.

Even the youngest pupils can be encouraged to develop an opinion about simple issues that affect them. Senior classes may also use discussion to develop ideas that can be used in composition writing.

Getting ideas

You might want to develop a discussion on **'Roads'.** There are many issues that could be included. Use **brainstorming** to get pupils to contribute ideas.

The ideas that the pupils suggested

Getting to school
Flooding after the rains
Cars and lorries
Journeys to other towns
Bicycles
Road names and signposts
Traffic on the roads
ROADS
Motorways
People selling things at the side or in the middle of the road
People walking along the road
Traffic policemen
Building new roads
Dust during the dry season
Road accidents

Finding and presenting information

- Involve the whole class in the discussion by giving different groups one of the themes to think about for 10 minutes. Help each group develop their ideas for a short presentation.
- Allow each group two or three minutes to present their information to the others. Try to encourage all members of the group to take part in the presentation and to provide an opportunity for questions or comments from other groups.
- You can use written work to summarise the discussion.

> ***Activity*** *Local or school issues that could be debated*
>
> A library or a Science laboratory – which would be of greater benefit to pupils in our school?
>
> Are there any parents who might like to be involved in this activity?

Debating

A debate is a formal way of discussing issues and is more suitable for older pupils. It is one way of involving the older pupils in thinking about the development of the school.

You might organise a debate in your own class, as a cross-curricular activity with other classes in your school (or with other schools in your cluster).

Organising a debate

If your pupils have not taken part in a debate before, it is better for you to act as the chairperson, at least for the first time, so that you can make the rules of debating quite clear.

Timing

Pupils should be given ten to fifteen minutes to prepare their speeches.

Let the groups choose speakers to present their argument. The main speakers, e.g. one speaking in favour of a library for the school and one speaking in favour of a Science laboratory should be allowed to speak for two minutes. One seconder speaks in support of each of the main speakers. They are allowed two minutes each (a total of eight to ten minutes).

After listening to the main speeches pupils are allowed to ask questions or make comments of their own. This question period should last for four or five minutes. When they want to speak, pupils should be encouraged to raise a hand. They should not to call out or interrupt another person.

At the end of the discussion/question time the main speakers are allowed one minute each to summarise their argument.

Everyone in the audience then votes for the argument they found most convincing.

28 Problem-solving activities

Activity *More Maths problems to solve*

Begin by putting a **solved** problem on the board. Then put two or three similar problems on the board for the pupils to solve. You may find that they are more successful if they work in a group.

Start 20
(divide by 2)
(subtract 4)
The answer is ?

Now let pupils solve these, then make up four examples of their own. Exchange these in the groups.

Start ?
(add 6)
(multiply by 4)
The answer is 56

Start ?
(divide by 10)
(subtract 5)
The answer is 1

Can your pupils explain **the rule** for solving these problems?

Pupils should be encouraged to develop a sense of enquiry and try to discover for themselves why things work in a particular way. They should learn to ask if things could work just as well in another way. Problem-solving is an activity that cuts across the curriculum and can be part of work on language, Mathematics, Social or Environment studies, Science or Technology. Many classroom activities are designed to find a solution to a task set either in the textbook or by the teacher. These tasks, however, do not necessarily develop the skills specifically required to solve problems.

What is the difference?

Text book exercises usually test one particular part of a subject the pupils have been studying, like finding the answer to 4×30. Pupils need to use their imagination and to think in a different way if they want to solve a problem.

You may find this type of problem in your Mathematics textbook. What number begins in the start box? If you can solve this problem – make up some more examples of your own.

Start	(add 4)	(multiply by 3)	The answer is 36
e.g.8	(8 + 4)	(12 × 3)	36

Pupils who have had practice with the kind of problem illustrated will be able to solve it quite easily by themselves.

Some pupils will need to listen to an explanation of the problem. They may need some practice with simple numbers until they gain confidence (see examples in the margin).

Problem solving is about learning to work systematically

Steps in problem solving

This can take a lot of patience and time.

- Always make sure that your pupils understand the question.
- Taking the first steps in trying to find a solution to a problem can be difficult. Ask pupils to look for clues in the information provided.
- Some activities may have several possible solutions. Encourage groups to look for alternative solutions.
- See if they can work out a rule for solving the problem. Does it always work?

Activity *Real life situations and Science*

- Find the best way of keeping something cool without a fridge.
- How can you stop food from going bad if you do not have a fridge?
- What problems would you like to be able to solve?

Setting up problem-solving activities across the curriculum

In some cases problems may be related to a particular lesson, others might be related to real life situations. Often they can be both. (See also Puzzles, Topic 46.)

Maths

- Use a table to work out how many different sets of uniforms you can make with these clothes:
  blue skirt, white blouse, black socks
  brown skirt, blue blouse, white socks
- Try to work it out using cut-out pictures that you can move about.

Technology

1 As part of a project on Flight or Weather, ask groups to design and make a kite using local materials.
- Fly the kites on a windy day. Record the results in a table or some other agreed way. (Which kite flew highest; which stayed up longest.)
- Fly the kites in different types of weather. When will they not fly at all?

2 Which group can make the **tallest** shape that will stand by itself from an empty cement bag or from two sheets of newspaper?

Evaluating solutions

Evaluating problem-solving activities is not easy. Often pupils can evaluate the different solutions themselves but you may need to give some kind of grade or comment as part of your continuous assessment records. Your mark can be based on your observations within the groups.

- Who thinks of the ideas?
- Did individuals or the group make use of drawings or notes to find a solution?
- Did pupils work well together, listening and offering suggestions?
- Which pupils avoid participating?
- Who made sure that the work was completed successfully and clearly presented?

29 Successful learning

There is an old saying: *You can take a camel to water but you cannot make it drink: a teacher can organise the lesson but cannot make pupils learn* and yet this is one of the most important tasks that teachers have to do. Every lesson is gradually built up in stages. This topic will concentrate on achieving **successful learning.**

The steps that must be taken by teachers and pupils to achieve successful learning show that there is no quick way to the top, and no step that can be ignored. Every lesson is built up in stages.

Planning and presentation are the all important first steps. Topic 16, Preparation and planning, Topic 18, Lesson plans and Topic 19, Lesson presentation skills will help you as teacher to focus on these.

Once you have presented the lesson you need to help your pupils learn the lesson successfully by giving them opportunities to **practise** the skills and knowledge they have learned.

What can a teacher can do to improve learning?

There are a number of ways that you can help pupils **remember** the information and learn to use it in a variety of different ways.

Sometimes the knowledge and skills have to be **reinforced** by you and your pupils together.

- Do the pupils really **understand** what they are learning?
- Can they **transfer** that knowledge and use it in another way?

Activity *Helping pupils learn*

Which of the following do you use most?

- I explain the topic and give them notes to learn.
- I ask questions during the lesson to see if they can **remember** facts and information.
- Pupils do exercises from the textbook.
- I give extra practical activities of my own.
- I give homework
- They do corrections when the work is wrong

> ***Activity*** *Improving memory recall*
>
> - Play memory games, like **I went to market** in which each pupil adds another item to the list. (Pupil 1:I went to market and I bought some yams. Pupil 2: I went to market and I bought some yams and a pepper.)
> - **Kim's game** is another useful game for improving recall. About twenty items are put on a tray or table. The pupils are given one minute to try to memorise them. The items are then covered or removed and the pupils write down as many as they can remember.
>
> If you have already used Topic 20, Planning outside visits, ask the pupils if they can remember the safety/commonsense rules.

> *Examples of transfer of learning*
>
> - Writing a letter of application for a job.
> - Using graphs to study traffic.
> - Calculating the rise in the price of food in the market using (Averages and percentages).

Ways to reinforce learning

- Provide immediate and continuous feedback.
  In order to maintain their interest pupils need to know whether they have solved a problem correctly. Always go over exercises with them as soon as possible. Correcting mistakes is useful and also helps motivate pupils.
- Link information to other known facts. Some pupils may be unable to recall a piece of information but will recognise the correct answer in a multiple choice question.
- Revision. Revise frequently. Do not leave revision until the end of the term. The process can become repetitive and boring. Use the idea of a **web** or a **network diagram** (see Topic 48, Project work) to help students link vocabulary or ideas together.

Transfer of learning

When pupils develop the ability to transfer knowledge they have acquired in one lesson and use it in other (real-life) situations they will have acquired **meaningful learning**.

Conditions that can help or hinder learning in the classroom

Learning is not just a matter of (cognitive processing) being able to memorise information and recall facts.

Learning is a social activity

Children learn best when they can share experiences with other pupils in the class and with their teacher. Different types of group activities and class discussion play a much more important part in our lessons nowadays.

Children need to feel that their teacher has confidence in them

Remember to praise success. It increases motivation and pupils will want to learn more. Pupils who are humiliated in class or who are afraid of their teacher may learn something by heart for a short time but will never progress beyond that level of learning.

Children will only learn when they are ready and want to learn

Motivation plays an important part in successful learning. The resource materials that you use, and the way you present your lesson can all increase the motivation and learning levels of your pupils.

30 Praise and punishment

Activity *Which of the following types of pupil behaviour do you praise most often?*

- Perseverance – even if the answers are not entirely correct.
- Progress in relation to past work.
- Achieving high scores in class work or tests.
- Original thinking.
- Using imagination/being creative.
- Neatness/careful work.
- Willingness to do classroom tasks.
- Good social behaviour (politeness, following rules, being helpful in class).

Activity *What rewards do you use in your class?*

- Stars and Merit Points (for both groups and individuals).
- Each group is given a jar: pupils put a bean or small stones into their jar for good work. The class or group is allowed to do something they like to do when the jar is full.
- Do something that pupils enjoy at the end of the day (read a story, or organise a quiz or a game).
- Put work on display.
- Allow the pupil to carry out a task which everyone likes doing.

A high standard of pupil motivation and behaviour is regarded as one of the most important measures of a good school. Teachers, like parents, need to be aware of a variety of strategies that can help them attain these goals.

Praise and rewards

Genuine praise and encouragement are positive methods that can be used to encourage a feeling of self-confidence and achievement and also to improve attitudes and change pupils' behaviour. Let each one know that you are interested in him/her. Make sure that you learn everyone's name as soon as possible at the beginning of the term. Smile and speak in a friendly way and let pupils know that you really value their contributions.

How should praise be used?

Always praise or punish the behaviour, not the child. **You have got all of these correct** rather than **Good boy or girl**.

1. Praise something specific rather than make a general comment: **You have used some very interesting words in that story** rather than **That is a good story**.
2. Even where an answer may be wrong, indicate the part that is correct and then suggest looking at the part that needs correction. **You have got the sum right as far as this but there is a mistake in the last part of the addition** or **You have used the right method but you need to check this part again**.
3. Good work should be pinned up for others to see but also needs comment. **This has given a lot of new information about....** or **Very neat, clear diagrams.**

Ways of using praise to change behaviour

Find something to say to a pupil who is misbehaving without actually mentioning the bad behaviour: **Elizabeth can you find the exercise that you got full marks for yesterday?** Praise another group that is behaving correctly: **I am glad to see that the red table has settled down to work so quickly.**

Activity *Attitudes to punishment.*

Which statement expresses your feeling best?

I believe in being very strict. You have to maintain discipline and show that you are in authority.

I believe pupils want to behave well. They sometimes make mistakes. They need clear guidance.

I think it is better to encourage pupils to change rather than punish them for every instance of bad behaviour.

If you let pupils get away with bad behaviour others will follow their example. The cane may be painful but it teaches a lesson and shows others what will happen if they break rules.

I am not sure that caning or being made to kneel in front of the class teaches anything but fear. It certainly does not seem to make a lasting improvement in behaviour or on learning.

Discuss your views with other teachers or student teachers.

Punishment

Teachers like parents may feel that punishment is a necessary part of helping children to learn how to behave. The punishments allowed in a particular school may be part of a Disciplinary Code approved by the Ministry of Education but some schools may have their own 'Code of Conduct' decided on by a Board of Governors, or the School Management Committee.

Activity *What punishments do you find most effective?*

Making a pupil sit in the front or at the back of the class.

Reprimands, like 'Stop talking and get on with your work'.

Making a pupil stand in the corner, facing the wall or outside the classroom.

Making a pupil stay in at playtime or miss the games/physical education lesson.

Giving extra work in Mathematics or sweeping.

Making a pupil pick up litter.

Giving detention after school.

Physical punishment such as caning or kneeling.

Sending a pupil to the head teacher.

Writing a letter to parents.

Making remarks that insult or make fun of the pupil concerned.

Punishing the whole class even if only one or two pupils were involved.

Which ones do you use regularly?

Which ones do you think might have the opposite effect to the one intended?

Never act in haste or as a result of losing your temper.

Don't let the sun go down on an argument.

31 Extra-curricular activities

Activity

Which of the following are available in the school you are in?

- 'Child to Child' activities or The Red Cross Society.
- Girl Guides or Boy Scouts.
- A School Choir or a School Band.
- Special Interest clubs such as gardening, animal rearing, health or craft clubs.

Does your school join other schools for:

- Sports or games competitions?
- Music, drama or cultural festivals?
- Religious festivals?

Does the school take part in special ceremonies such as Independence Day or hold a Speech Day or an Open Day?

Why does your school consider that activities like these are important?

Which activities do you help with?

Many schools feel that instruction is only a part of the overall education of children. They like to encourage their pupils to be involved in activities that take place outside the official school time. These are called extra-curricular activities.

There are a number of reasons why it is important to encourage pupils to join in extra-curricular or co-curricular activities.

- **Child development**

Several of the activities mentioned teach valuable life-skills: First aid, health awareness, Arts and Craft, or Music and Dancing.

- **Physical and social development**

Practising to compete in district or regional sports and games competitions develops physical fitness and mental alertness. The competitions themselves may take pupils to another school, or your school may host visiting teams. These opportunities develop social skills – pupils learn how to make guests feel welcome or to congratulate the winning team when their team has lost a competition or an important match.

- **Developing self-esteem and a sense of pride in the school**

Any performance, whether it is a gymnastic or cultural display or a display of work for Open Day is the result of many hours of work by teachers and pupils. Some pupils who are otherwise poor students may excel at this kind of activity. Their increased self-esteem may encourage them to improve their academic work as well.

Schools that perform well in competitions are usually mentioned on the radio or TV news and there is often an article in the local newspaper. This also gives parents and the comunity a sense of pride in their school.

What are the problems in providing a programme of extra-curriculur activities?

- **Finding time**

Schools operating on a double-shift system face particular difficulties. Most activities need at least one hour if pupils are to develop their interests.

Schools on the morning shift usually end at noon. Extra-curricular activities have to take place between 12:15 and 1:15 pm, before the afternoon shift begins. This is the hottest part of the day and outside activities will be difficult for both pupils and teachers. Schools on the afternoon shift arrange their extra-curricular activities between 4.30 and 5:30 pm. However, some pupils have to walk two or three miles to their homes. Many will be unable to stay after school as it gets dark soon after 5:30 pm at certain times of the year.

> ### *Activity*
>
> - **Finding funds**
>
> During the term many activities require very little money but funds may be needed if your school wants to enter competitions or to put on a performance during an Open Day. Sports teams may need a special uniform or a cultural troupe may need costumes. This is where you will need to work with the PTA, the School Management Committee or to make an appeal to local business people. After a match or performance the uniforms or costumes should be washed and stored carefully ready for the next performance.

Some alternatives that different schools have used.

- School A holds extra-curricular activities very early in the morning before school starts officially.
- School B holds activities during an extended break time in the middle of the official school-time.
- Schools C and D, while operating a double shift, decided to hold activities for both shifts between 12.15 and 1.15 pm. They found teachers from both the morning and afternoon shifts were willing to work together.

Extra-curricular activities and teachers

Primary school teachers usually have very little free time and yet many enjoy taking extra-curricular activities. Why?

I have always enjoyed sports activities and like to see teams from my school do well in local and regional competitions.

When I was in school we had a school band. At festival time we marched through the town. It made us feel so proud to see everyone line the street to listen to us. I want to make people proud of this school too.

I enjoy the opportunity to get to know pupils from other classes. I work with one of the parents and we teach pupils how to make baskets and bags.

32 Working with the whole class

> ***Activity*** *When do you use whole class teaching?*
>
> - To introduce a new topic?
> - To explain how activities or projects will be done?
> - To give out homework assignments?
> - To practise learning (such as reciting tables or poems)?
> - To summarise learning at the end of a lesson?
> - Story time?

Whole class teaching is often linked to a traditional or formal approach to teaching. This method is sometimes criticised as being **teacher-centred** because it places the teacher in control of the learning process. Initial teacher training courses now lay emphasis on **child-centred** approaches that make more use of activities and group work. Recent research has shown, however, that within most lesson plans there is a place for some whole class teaching. For many teachers it may be the most effective way of teaching large classes where few pupils have access to a textbook and there are very few resources.

Using whole class teaching

Beginning and ending lessons

There are times when all the pupils should pay attention to what the teacher is saying. At the beginning of the lesson you need to establish control by making sure that pupils are ready to work. Are they clear about the objectives of the lesson? Towards the end of each lesson you will need a few minutes to summarise the learning and focus everyone's attention on what will happen next or on homework that needs to be done.

Introducing a new topic

Even though you may have planned to involve pupils in group activities or individual work later in the lesson, it is a good idea to introduce a new topic to the whole class. This allows you to gain everyone's attention and interest and to find out what pupils already know. (See Topic 19, Lesson presentation skills.)

Giving instructions

After the introduction, the lesson will proceed more smoothly if pupils are clear about the work they will have to do. Before starting group or individual activities, take a few minutes to give instructions to the whole class. Explain what each group will do: Where will they sit, if you want them to move from their normal seating area? What resources will they need and where will they find them? How long do they have to complete the tasks? How do you want the work to be presented? If this is clear from the beginning there will be more time to answer individual queries.

Reinforcing learning

For teachers with very large classes, whole class teaching is one of the most useful ways of making sure that all pupils have a chance to practise new material and reinforce earlier learning. (See Topic 29, Successful learning.) Some teachers ask pupils to memorise and recite tables, or to practise language skills by speaking together. The main problem about this method is that, after a while, pupils no longer think about the numbers or the words they are reciting. Try to vary the method by making this kind of learning into a team game.

Questions and answers

Provide an opportunity for pupils to ask and answer questions. Choose an activity and discuss the kind of questions that they might ask to find out about the topic.

A visit to a lake/a large river or the sea

What can we see along the edge of the water?
Did you see any boats?
What did they look like?
Did you see any fishermen?
What were they doing?

Pupils can also ask questions about a school sports day, a traditional festival, a religious festival, a long journey or a football match for this activity.

What are the particular problems you need to think about?

The level of learning

When teaching the whole class, your lessons will have to provide information and activities that most pupils can do. This may not be appropriate for pupils at either the top or the bottom end of the ability range. Bright pupils will probably finish assignments quickly and then become bored or badly behaved whilst pupils with low ability may feel that they can never succeed.

The level of pupil involvement

If you are teaching the whole class together you will need to pay particular attention to the level of pupil involvement. During question time, for example, you will have noticed that some pupils always want to give the answers. There are others who never volunteer, even if they know an answer. Make sure that everyone has a chance to make a contribution at some point in the lesson.

Changing your focus

You may also find that unconsciously you talk to a particular area of the room and to those pupils who are taking an active interest in the lesson. There may be others, sitting on the side or right at the back who can easily be overlooked or forgotten. Make a conscious effort to focus on different groups by moving your position or your gaze from time to time.

Activity *Reinforcing language skills*

Examples

How many adjectives can they use to describe an object? Work quickly round the class.

- **My book is**: a *red* book/an *old* book/a *torn* book/a *story* book/an *interesting* book/a *school* book. Change the word when it looks as though pupils are running out of ideas.
- **What will I be when I grow up?** (Each word must use the **er** ending.)

I will be a *writer:* a *singer,* a *miner*, a *farmer*, a *teacher*, a *drummer*, a *carpenter.*

33 Group work

Group work is a less formal, child-centred, method of teaching. Primary teachers are encouraged to use groups in a variety of different situations, both as a way of managing a large class and as a learning process. Group work requires quite different skills from those in other teaching situations.

Different ways of grouping pupils

- **Ability groups**

Generally used for subjects such as number work or reading.

- **Activity groups**

For registration, or special activities such as physical education, drama or traditional music and dancing.

- **Age groups**

Used in schools with very few pupils where two or three grades have to be taught by the same teacher.

- **Interest/friendship groups**

Often mixed ability groups, e.g. for art and craft or where pupils are interested in preparing a particular topic for a class project.

- **Gender groups**

In some schools boys and girls are grouped separately as it is considered inappropriate to have mixed groups.

What is the value of group work?

It is generally believed that if the lesson is carefully prepared, the members of small groups of between four to eight pupils can achieve several things.

- Development of social skills; learning to work together.
- Increased independence; individuals learn that they do not necessarily have to ask the teacher what to do next.
- Increased levels of understanding; pupils learn to talk to each other about the planning and management of set tasks and the content of the lesson.

Group work or working in groups?

What are your pupils doing?

Are pupils in your class working together to complete a task or are they simply sitting in groups but working as individuals? Placing children around a table does not mean that they will work as a group. You will need to provide special guidance if groups are to work together effectively. They will need to be given opportunities to explore ideas, share experiences and learn to work with others.

Successful group work

All group activities need careful planning and preparation so that they relate to the learning objectives of the lesson. Give clear instructions before work begins and make sure that each group knows what it has to find out and how long the activity should take. **You have ten minutes to complete this task and at the end of that time, I would like the leaders to….**

Monitoring group activities

As you move around the class, spend a few minutes observing each group. Make a note of any problems or good ideas and use these observations in your summary of the learning at the end of the lesson. Make sure that at some point during the day each member of each group has an opportunity to make a contribution to the lesson.

ACTIVITY

Groups in your class

How are groups chosen in your class?

Do you make changes for different subjects or activities?

Getting the right group mixture

Inappropriate group mixtures can lead to problems in class management.

Problems may develop if pupils always work with the same ability group. They very quickly know whether they are in the highest or the lowest group.

Pupils always assigned to groups of low achievers may gradually give up. They need the stimulation of working with good students.

Learning achievement is often improved (at least for some lessons or subjects) if there is a mixture of ability within each group.

You may find that single sex groups are more appropriate in your area or for particular lessons but, if possible, encourage boys and girls to work together at least some of the time.

What skills do pupils need?

Pupils will need good communication skills. They need to be able to listen, question, explain, give an opinion and learn to accept other opinions. Group work can help less confident pupils to develop these skills.

What are the difficulties?

In all classes, there are pupils who do not work well within a group. One or two pupils may dominate or girls may be reluctant to take a lead. Give responsibility for co-ordinating some activities to less dominant individuals and make sure that the group leader changes occasionally. Monitor the way pupils interact within their group and make adjustments where necessary.

Preparation for group work

Lesson preparation requires a lot of thought as group work sometimes means increased levels of noise in the class. Pupils should be able to talk about their work or move from one task to another but they will need to understand the level of noise and movement that is acceptable to you. Prepare extra resources, work cards or supplementary exercises to keep everyone busy.

Rotating groups

This arrangement has proved very useful where there are no desks and where resources are scarce. It is particularly successful with lower primary classes in both reading and number work. It can also be used as a teaching strategy in large classes or mixed-age classes. See Topic 13, Managing large classes and Topic 12, Mixed-ability and mixed-age classes.

Different practical or written activities can be set up in a semi-circle on mats around the room. One group is assigned to each mat. The teacher works with the group on one mat. After four or five minutes, each group moves to the next mat. The teacher stays where he/she is. A well-prepared teacher has an opportunity to monitor the progress of each group and each individual within each group during the lesson.

34 Working in pairs

Studies have shown that working with a partner is a very effective method of learning even in large classes.

What is its value?

Reasons for using pair grouping

- To increase the level of activity in the class.

One of your concerns as a teacher is to make sure that most pupils in your class are actively involved in the lesson. (See Topic 33, Group work for an example of pupils who are seated in groups though not everyone is working. Certain pupils seem to take the lead whilst others may sit very quietly copying the answers.)

- To increase the level of learning.

Studies show that partners learn more if they are given opportunities to share, discuss and challenge each other's ideas.

- To improve the learning of weaker pupils.

This kind of pairing is often called **peer-tutoring.**

- To improve pupils' communications skills, e.g. **listening** then **relaying**; **talking** then **explaining**; **giving instructions**, **questioning**, **persuading**; **thinking** skills: **categorising**, **getting information** from a text on picture, **analysing** and **comparing**.

What kind of pairing can be used?

Apart from friendship there are a variety of combinations that can be used successfully. These are illustrated in the box.

Activity *Which are the best partnerships?*

In the list below there are several 'partnerships' that you might use. When would you use each of the following?

- Two pupils of the same sex?
- Two pupils who are normally very quiet and do not take a very active role in a larger mixed group?
- Two able pupils?
- An able pupil and a weaker pupil?
- An older pupil and a younger pupil?

What kind of lessons provide the best opportunities for pairing?

- Language lessons to practise speaking and listening skills.
- English to improve reading and comprehension skills or to work out ideas for a composition.
- Maths or Science allowing partners to work together on practical activities such as analysing a soil sample or recording data.
- Project work.
- Physical Education.

English/or local language lessons

Conversation lessons, in particular, provide a number of opportunities for paired work. For example, pupils might practise greetings, asking and answering questions or giving directions.

Some conversation exercises should be **structured.** As part of the activity you can provide examples of conversations for pupils to practise. To save time you can write sample questions on cards.

Examples of pair work

- Practise the correct way to greet people or introduce one person to another.
- Use unfinished sentences. Partners find a suitable ending to a number of sentences:

  'My teacher asked me if ....'

  'When I went home yesterday....'
- Help pupils to develop free conversation. Agree on a theme and partners can then develop their own conversation on it.
- Interview your partner. Each child writes five questions they want their partner to ask them (personal likes and dislikes, friends, music or hobbies). They then exchange sheets and interview each other.

  Conversations can be monitored easily as you move around the class. This can help pupils learn an interview technique.

Physical education

- Use pairs to improve observation skills.
  One partner carries out a simple movement (stretching, standing on one leg or jumping over a stone). The partner **observes** the movement and then **copies** it exactly.
- The leader carries out a short **sequence** of movements. The partner must do the same movements as they are being done. (Examples: Raise one hand slowly into the air, lower it. Spin round and then fall down to the floor.)
- Partners can think of ways that they can use their weight to make an interesting shapes based on **balance** and **support**.

Peer tutoring

Peer tutoring is an approach that partners a more able pupil with another who has particular learning difficulties. This method is useful in improving learning in both Reading and Mathematics. Whilst more able students should not be asked to help students with learning problems too often, peer tutoring can be of benefit to both partners.

- Explaining how to do something to a partner, often helps to reinforce the learning of the tutor pupil.
- An explanation by a partner may be easier to understand for a weaker pupil than that given by the teacher during the lesson.
- Topic 38, Remedial teaching provides guidelines for helping with reading difficulties. These should be carefully explained to peer tutoring pupils.

Peer tutoring should take no more than 10 to 15 minutes, two or three times a week. This type of help can be given during the lunch-break or after school on certain days. Pairs may choose to work outside the classroom. Alternatively you could use a lesson at the end of the week.

35 Helping individual pupils

> ### *Activity* Educational needs
>
> This list below contains a variety of pupil needs teachers have identified:
>
> - Security, happiness and success.
> - To understand themselves.
> - To learn to make personal decisions and become less dependent on others.
> - To learn to co-operate with others.
> - To understand class rules and routines.
> - To acquire positive learning attitudes.
> - To develop language skills through reading and writing.
> - To acquire mathematical skills.
> - To be able to reason.
> - To be creative.
> - To be able to acquire knowledge and discover things for themselves.
> - To acquire cultural and artistic values.
> - To develop moral values.
> - To understand their environment.
> - To develop mental and physical co-ordination.
>
> Are there any others that you think are important that have been left out of the list?

Educational objectives outlined in the primary syllabus often refer to the personal development of children and the need to help them become useful members of society. This means that you need to be able to create a variety of learning opportunities that suit different learning styles. (See The process of learning, Topic 4.)

Identifying individual needs

The list opposite, which might also be found in the long-term educational goals identified by your ministry, should help you to identify the particular needs of each pupil in your class. These might be recorded in the following way.

Name of pupil	Personal needs
Robert	1 to improve mathematical skills 2 to learn to co-operate with others 3 to develop self-confidence
Ama	1 to develop language skills 2 to become less dependent on others and learn to make personal decisions. 3 to be more creative.

It is important to understand that, in any class, each pupil will have a different approach to learning.

Pupils are also different in their approach to life in the classroom.

The teacher's role in helping individuals

In your class there will be some pupils with learning difficulties and others who are more able or gifted. (See Topic 37, Special educational needs and Topic 36, Stretching able children.) Good teachers spend a lot of their time talking about both academic and personal matters with their pupils. This is an important element of effective teaching and develops the personal relationship between the teacher and each pupil. Recent studies have emphasised the importance of helping pupils develop self confidence and self-respect.

> ### *Activity* *Identifying the individual needs of pupils in my class*
>
> Use the list outlined above to find two needs that you would like to develop in each of your pupils over the next year.

How can this be done?

Correcting mistakes

The way that mistakes are corrected can do much to build or destroy self-confidence. It is nearly always possible to find at least some part of an answer that is correct. Identify this section and help the pupil recheck the work from that point.

Avoid comparisons

Comparing a poor student with other more clever members of the class, or members of their family, results in a sense of failure. Where teachers obviously expect a high level of achievement from pupils they generally respond to the challenge. Make sure that there are some learning activities that even the weakest pupil can do correctly.

Keep records to help identify individual problems

The records below show two ways that you might record information about your pupils

Pupil personality

Pupils are different in their approach to life in the classroom.

Can you identify particular pupils who:	**Names of pupils**
• constantly seek attention from you	
• prefer to be on their own	
• prefer to be with a group	
• find it difficult to make friends	
• never volunteer to answer questions	

Approaches to learning

It is also important to understand that each pupil has a different approach to learning.

Activity **Can you identify pupils who seem to learn most effectively when they:**	**Names of pupils**
• can read about the topic?	
• can hear an explanation either from the teacher or a member of their group?	
• have time to think about the information?	
• do practical activities?	
• have material that is illustrated with interesting pictures and diagrams?	

Records such as these should enable you to identify particular areas where individuals need help and they provide you with the information you need to be able to offer positive help. They can be used both to identify personal needs and as part of a continuous assessment.

36 Stretching able children

> ***Activity** Identifying gifted pupils*
>
> Think about the pupils in your class. Which ones show one or more of the following characteristics?
>
> - Particularly quick at learning new work.
> - Usually comes top of the class in tests and examinations.
> - Finishes assignments very quickly.
> - Is very good at one or perhaps two subjects but shows very little interest in others.
> - Learned to read or understand numbers at an early age.
> - Is curious and asks a lot of questions.
> - Has lots of ideas.

One of the most difficult tasks facing primary teachers is to find ways of meeting the learning needs of all the pupils in their class. Most teachers are able to prepare lessons or activities suited to the majority of pupils in the class. Many are able to recognise and respond to learning difficulties. However, the very gifted or able students are often neglected. Teachers expect them to do well and may give them less attention than other pupils in the class.

All pupils need a curriculum that is challenging and supportive. There is a concern that able or gifted pupils, in particular, are not sufficiently stretched by the teaching they normally experience in class.

Recognising able or gifted pupils

It is not always easy to recognise gifted pupils without using some of the specially designed tests available. However, in your daily observations of pupils you will probably have identified some pupils that you feel are very gifted.

Some of the pupils you have identified will have a high general academic **ability** in a range of subjects across the curriculum. There may be others who may have special **aptitude** in one particular subject area. They may be very talented in Athletics, Music, Art, or Mathematics but may not necessarily perform as well in other areas of the curriculum.

Meeting the needs of able pupils

Gifted pupils need a curriculum that allows them not only to study a particular subject in greater depth but also to work in areas not normally covered by the primary curriculum. It is not an easy task to provide for these special needs. You may have noticed several things about these pupils.

- Many gifted pupils are able to work for long periods by themselves if the topic is sufficiently interesting.
- They will often finish normal class activities very quickly. If there is nothing to keep them occupied they may then become bored and this can lead to behavioural problems or to low levels of achievement.

It is not enough to give them more examples of the same work. They need more challenging work.

Schools have used several approaches in their efforts to provide programmes that are sufficiently challenging.

Acceleration

This allows the pupil either to skip a class (e.g. move from Class 2 into Class 4) or to work with a higher class in certain subjects. For example, a child in Class 4 with a particular talent for Maths might work with pupils in Class 5 or 6.

Enrichment

Extends the pupil's education beyond the normal curriculum by providing more advanced information and activities or increasing the pace at which the pupil works. For example, provide more difficult reading material such as newspaper articles about, e.g. The environment. Ask the pupil to find out specific information and then to write an article or talk to the whole class.

Differentiation

Different tasks are set for different levels of achievement. (This approach has also been used to cater for pupils with learning difficulties.) In the case of more able pupils, this may mean that the pupil does more difficult tasks or that he or she does the same work as the rest of the class but is expected to produce more detailed answers.

The role of teachers

Even in schools with very limited resources it is possible to stretch able pupils.

- Allow them to work independently at their own pace.
- Give them more challenging tasks.
- Provide them with more difficult creative or problem-solving exercises.
- Allow them to work with other more able or perhaps older pupils.
- Provide them with work that will take them outside the limits of the classroom.

Let gifted pupils know that you expect answers of a high standard from them. This is particularly important if you have some who you feel are not working to the best of their ability.

Above all: Plan ahead.

Activity *What are the main problems?*

- Think about the three approaches used to help able pupils.
- Make a list of the main problems you think you would have to face in trying to adopt these methods.
- Discuss the problems with other teachers or student teachers. Have they used any of these?
- Which do you think is the most realistic approach for you or other teachers in your school?

Activity *Using projects*

Look at the project on 'Water' (Topic 48, Project work) or the suggestions made in Topic 57, Using the school compound. Try to develop activities for more able pupils using each of the following strategies. Some examples are suggested.

Independent work
Study a local stream or river
Finding Out Topics
Water pollution
Design
Design and make a weather station
Areas in which pupils could work with a higher class

37 Special educational needs

Almost all teachers can identify certain pupils in their class as slow learners who have problems with their work. There are others with poor attitudes to school or behaviour problems. These are pupils who have special educational needs.

Learning difficulties

What to look for

In general children with special needs show some or all of these characteristics.

- Poor motivation.
- A short span of attention.
- Poor memory.
- A poor vocabulary.
- Low attainment in reading or writing.
- Feel they cannot succeed.

Activity *Preparing a form to help you identify pupils with special educational needs.*

The comments in columns A and B are the kind that teachers use in their term reports.

A tick in column 1 would suggest that Statement **A** is true most of the time.

A tick in column 2 would suggest that Statement **B** is true most of the time.

Pupils with a majority of ticks in columns 2 may have special educational needs. Name: __________

	A	1	2	B
1	Enjoys new tasks and is eager to learn.			Shows little interest or motivation.
2	Concentrates on tasks.			Is easily distracted.
3	Perseveres with difficult work.			Becomes impatient and gives up easily.
4	Generally happy and cheerful.			Is often anxious or worried.
5	Enjoys meeting new people or working in a new situation.			Does not respond easily to new situations.
6	Sociable and friendly.			Does not make friends easily.
7	Even-tempered and easy-going.			Often irritable and quarrelsome.
8	Helpful and considerate towards others.			Can be a bully or spiteful towards others.
9	Readily accepts discipline and control.			Frequently disruptive, uncooperative and disobedient.
10	Will work independently.			Requires constant attention.

How can you help?

There are a number of practical ways that pupils with learning difficulties can be helped. (See Remedial teaching, Topic 38.)

Provide reassurance

Many pupils with learning difficulties lack confidence in their ability and feel that they are failures. They will need reassurance and may need more attention from you or to be helped by other members of their group. (See Working in pairs, Topic 34.)

Provide learning opportunities that suit their particular approach to learning

It is important to find out their approach to learning (See Successful learning, Topic 29.) Children with learning difficulties often respond more positively to verbal instructions, to visual representations of material or to practical activities rather than to written work. They will also learn more easily through games. (See Working in pairs, Topic 34.)

Repetition

Ask questions that will require the learning information or instructions to be repeated. Provide a selection of simple activities that will repeat and reinforce the learning (See Successful learning, Topic 29.) You will need to talk to parents so that you can show them the help their child needs. (See Involving parents in school activities, Topic 68.)

Look for something positive

Last, but not least, every child has some good points. Improve the child's self-image by giving him/her a task that gives a sense of responsibility and provides an opportunity for success.

What causes learning difficulties?

There may be mental, social, emotional or physical reasons why a pupil may have difficulties in school.

- Language difficulties, particularly if a pupil does not speak the local language.
- Physical problems, such as bad eyesight or poor hearing.
- Poor health caused by malaria or malnutrition.
- Problems at home.

In some cases these difficulties may be temporary in nature. The pupil's health may improve or eyesight be improved by a pair of spectacles. Nevertheless you need to be aware of special needs and be ready to provide help.

What do I need to know in order to assess whether a pupil has learning difficulties?

- The rate of progress of that child in relation to others in the class. You may have recognised that certain pupils are much slower at grasping new work than the rest of the class.
- The level of attainment expected for most pupils in the class. Despite all your efforts there are probably some pupils who are unable to keep up with the learning achievements expected of their age group.
- There are areas that give an indication of learning difficulties.
  1. Oral communication skills and reading.
  2. Number skills.

How do I make the assessment?

Information needs to be gradually built up through daily observation and continuous assessment records.

Day to day evaluations

Is the child able to cope with lessons? Look for clues in:

- The child's behaviour.
- The child's answers to questions/daily class-work and tests.

Continuing assessment

Is the pupil able to keep up with the class? Look for clues in:

- End of term test marks.
- Termly report forms.

Reports from other teachers and/or a previous school may also be valuable sources of information.

38 Remedial teaching

> ### *Activity*
>
> In which areas of the curriculum do you find that pupils are most in need of remedial teaching?
>
> Try to assess **why** your pupils need remedial lessons.
>
> Make a list or a chart to help in your assessment.

Remedial teaching is the term used to describe the way that teachers try to help pupils who do not seem to have serious learning difficulties and yet are not achieving good results in school. Two groups of pupils have special needs that will often respond to remedial teaching. You may have some pupils like this in your class.

Pupils requiring special help

Under-achievers

These are pupils with ability, but who, for one reason or another do not achieve the results that you expect. Frequently, under-achievers lack motivation or find normal lessons too easy. Ideas to help this particular problem are detailed in Topic 29, Successful learning and Topic 36, Stretching able children.

Slow learners

Slow learners are pupils with low levels of ability who find difficulty learning and remembering. Other pupils may have particular learning problems. They may perform well in many areas of the curriculum, but have problems related to Spelling and Reading or Mathematics. Ideas to help this group can also be found in Topic 37, Special educational needs.

It is likely that you have identified the need for remedial reading classes. Teachers, in both primary and junior secondary schools, find that pupils who are not doing well in school are those who, for some reason, have never learned to read properly. An inability to read will affect levels of learning in most other subjects.

Remedial reading

Reading aloud in class can be a very painful experience for pupils who are poor readers. It rarely improves reading. Poor readers need regular help but this may not be possible if there are a large number of pupils in your class. In some schools the School Committee or the head teacher encourages parents to act as volunteer support staff for one or two hours each week. Alternatively you could ask good readers in your class to help. (See Working in pairs, Topic 34.) You will need to show helpers exactly how to work with poor readers. Arrange a timetable that will allow them to follow this step by step approach for 10 to 15 minutes, two or three times each week.

Choosing remedial reading material

You may feel that there are not enough books available in your class for reading practice. Try letting older pupils read the local paper or a magazine. They may also find it useful to read a chapter from one of the textbooks. The helper can then ask questions that will increase understanding of the topic.

Remedial reading step by step

- **Read together:** At first, pupil and helper read a short paragraph together, slowly, following the words with their fingers.
- **Read alone:** The pupil is then encouraged to read alone. If he/she comes to a word they cannot read, pause, giving the reader time to solve the problem.
- **Give help:** If the reader cannot go on, **give a clue**.
- Ask the reader for the initial sound of the word.
- Look at the picture on the page. This often gives an idea about the word.
- Ask a question about what has happened before in the passage. This often gives a clue.
- Read the rest of the sentence and then go back to the difficult word.
- **Praise** the reader if he/she can work out what the word is.
- **Tell:** After two tries, if the reader still cannot guess, tell him or her the word.
- **Read that sentence again.**
- **Finally let the reader read the paragraph again.**

Organising remedial activities

In the past, the approach to remedial subject teaching has been to give pupils extra exercises of the same type of work, rather than to find different ways of solving the problem. In order to give effective help to slow learners and pupils with particular learning difficulties, you need to think of new strategies that will improve learning achievements.

- Organise the class into small groups or pairs (two pupils with similar needs or a good student with a poor student).
- Make use of other people (older students in the school or other members of the community).
- Show family members how they can help.
- Try to find retired teachers or secondary school students who may be willing to spend a little time helping your pupils.
- Use games to improve memory, or drama to improve language skills.
- Help pupils talk through the process of working out an answer. Ask them, **What did you do? Why did you do that? Could it be done another way?**
- Make material adapted to the pupil's own special interests.
- Combine reading and writing with a project which involves making something.
- If you have access to a tape recorder, make tapes of the reading material so that the pupil can read and listen at the same time.
- Songs can be used to help reading. Write the words on a large sheet and point to them as the pupils sing.

Correcting mistakes

You may find that certain errors become part of the way pupils speak or write. (e.g. my *best* food instead of my *favourite* food). There are times, particularly in composition writing, when your pupils need to write spelling or grammar corrections.

The most effective way to do this is to make a circle around the word or phrase that is wrong and let pupils write it correctly on the **same line** in the margin. In that way the correct spelling or grammar becomes linked to its meaning and use. You can quickly check through their writing to see which errors continue to appear and note any improvement.

39 Choosing the best method

Teaching methods

Story-telling; drama, role-play, rhymes and songs.

Displays, pictures, flash cards and models.

Experiments, demonstrations, games, field trips, role-playing, making things.

Question and answer sessions; whole class teaching group work; pair work; projects. Class or group discussion.

Quizzes; find-out and problem-solving exercises

Why use different methods for teaching?

Pupils learn more effectively if you use a variety of teaching methods. (See Successful learning, Topic 29.) Each lesson should include the following.

- Spoken information.
- Supporting teaching and visual aids.
- Practical activities.
- Opportunities for discussion both teacher/pupil and pupil/pupil.
- Time for thinking and reflection.

In the first box you can see how each of these lesson activities can be linked to different teaching methods.

Choosing teaching methods

Before you choose a particular teaching method think about the knowledge and skills of your pupils, their ability and the kind of experience they can bring to the lessons. Textbooks may suggest certain methods for teaching topics within the syllabus, but this may not suit all pupils. You may find that you need to teach some of the topics in a different way.

You will probably find that you use some teaching methods far more frequently than others or that you use certain methods with particular subjects. For instance you may use drama or rhymes in English lessons but rarely in Social or Environment Studies. You may also find that you use drills in Mathematics but never in English. There may be some methods that you have never used at all.

Matching teaching methods and activities to lessons

It is very easy to use only the methods suggested in a textbook or workbook. Make a list of new methods and activities you might like to try and then match them to a lesson, for example, drama and mime can be used to extend the learning in language lessons, Health Studies and lessons on Citizenship.

Mini field trips

Use the school compound, a nearby farm or a local road for a simple **field trip**. In your planning think about all the possible cross-curriculum aspects of the trip.

- Pupils could be asked to look for shapes or angles (e.g. in buildings, cloth patterns, trees and vegetation) and these could be used to illustrate a Maths lesson.

Activity *Using different techniques*

How often do you use each of these techniques?

Talks by resource persons

Demonstration/experiments

Discussion

Role-play

Games and puzzles

Drama

Story-telling

Drills

Rhymes and songs

Question and answer/quizzes

Project work

Field trips

- As part of an Environmental Studies or Science project they might watch birds build nests, find out names of different plants, match trees and shrubs with their leaves, flowers, fruits and seeds, or measure the growth of crops.
- If a road runs along the boundary of your school compound pupils could count cars, bicycles, lorries and pedestrians. This information could be used in lessons on sets and graphs.

Talks

You might ask parents or members of the PTA to give a short talk to your pupils. Their knowledge of traditional crafts such as basket weaving, pottery or carving could contribute to Environment lessons or Social Studies. They might also be able to talk about local history. Explain to your visitor that the talk should not last more than 10 minutes and that you would like your pupils to be encouraged to ask questions and perhaps watch a demonstration of a local craft.

Drills

Some teaching methods are regarded as old-fashioned, but they can be effective, especially when you find yourself in a school with very few textbooks and large classes. Drills help pupils to memorise spelling or the correct use of grammar. Think of ways of turning drills into games.

Experiments and demonstrations

Teachers often feel it is impossible to carry out experiments if they do not have a Science lab or proper scientific equipment. There are many simple experiments, however, that can be carried out with a minimum of equipment. Use experiments and demonstrations in Science and Maths or as part of a study of your school compound or local area. (See Using the school compound, Topic 57, Using your local area, Topic 58, and Experiments and demonstrations, Topic 41.)

If you can be more imaginative in your choice of lesson material you will find that your classroom will become a more interesting place to work in. Lessons that always follow the same pattern become boring.

Make yourself a promise to try ONE new method each term.

40 Using textbooks

> ***Activity*** *Making a list of the core information in one unit of a textbook.*
>
> **Subject/Title of the Unit**:
> e.g. Primary English, Class 4
>
> Title.................................
>
> **The content of the unit.**
>
> This unit is a story/ information about................
>
> The main points are:
>
> The aim of the lesson is to develop skills in:

In many primary schools reference books and other supplementary material may be in very short supply. Subject textbooks may be the only books available for the preparation of lessons.

Textbooks as a resource

Textbooks present information in a certain way. They are usually divided into a series of units that should be covered during the year. Each unit covers a particular topic or theme and there will be a number of exercises and **Things to do**. This may seem to limit what you can do with the material but with a little thought you can make your lessons interesting and enjoyable even if you have no other sources of information.

Using textbooks for information

This topic will show you how to use the information in the textbook to give your pupils a greater variety of exercises and help them understand and remember the core points covered in the unit more easily. (See also Lesson plans, Topic 18.)

> **Before your lesson, read through the unit you are going to teach very carefully.**

In every unit, there will be a number of exercises and activities that are designed to help your pupils build on previous knowledge and improve their skills. For example, a unit in an English textbook will expect you to develop reading, comprehension, writing and oral work.

Developing your own material from the unit

Study the text in the unit.

- What links can be made with pupil's existing knowledge?
- Is there a simple experiment or demonstration that you could do?
- Is there any additional information that you could ask pupils to find out about as they read the unit?
- How can you give your pupils more **practical** exercises?
- What simple teaching aids can you or or your pupils make and use?
- How can you approach the material in the unit in a different way to add variety and develop skills?

Activity *Planning your lessons*

1 Make a list of the suggested exercises/activities in the unit you will teach:

- Do they give your pupils practice in the skills listed?
- Are there enough exercises?
- Can you use the same exercise in different ways?

2 Decide how many exercises/activities your pupils can do in the lesson time.

- How long will each exercise/activity take?

3 Decide how pupils will complete each of the suggested exercises/activities, e.g. as a class, in groups or in pairs.

- Do all the activities have to be completed in the classroom?
- Are there some activities that could make use of the school compound?

4 Make a list of the pictures used to illustrate the unit.

- How are they used in the unit?
- Can you use them in any other way?

Exercises and activities

In order to improve the level of learning in your class you will need to think of a variety of extra exercises that will give your pupils different ways of practising their skills.

Here are some examples

In a unit on Transport, exercises might ask pupils to **Look and Say**, to spell or to use words in the text in a sentence of their own. You can vary these exercises in a number of ways.

- Put the letters of words in a different order, e.g. leevich nocae intra (vehicle canoe train).
- Ask groups to make up riddles about the words.
- Find other words linked to one or more of the spelling words, e.g train linked words might be railway, ticket, passenger, luggage, etc. You could make this into a web diagram.

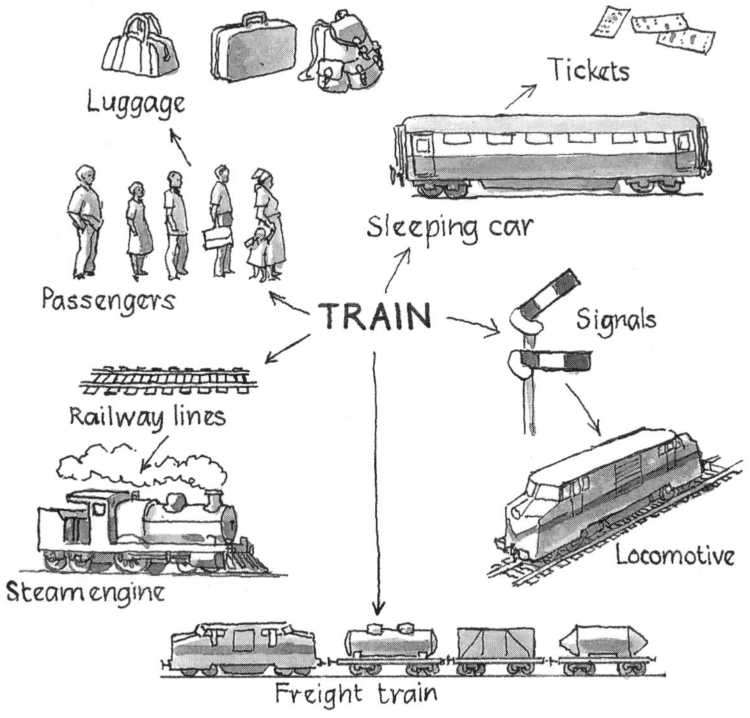

- Write a short story about **A Journey** using the words in the text together with the related words you discovered in the last exercise.

In other subjects look for opportunities to develop practical exercises. Link these to activities using the school compound (See Using the school compound, Topic 57.) Pupils can find their own resource material as part of the exercise, for example a collection of leaves could be used in lessons on symmetry, or a selection of stones or shells could be subdivided into sets.

41 Experiments and demonstrations

Activity *Planning and practice*

- Begin by going through the topic headings in one of your textbooks (perhaps, Social Studies or Science) and make a list of simple experiments or demonstrations you could do in at least two of the lessons that you have to teach over the next term.
- List the equipment either you or your pupils need to bring to school in order to do the demonstration. Make sure that all the equipment you need is ready and near your desk **before you begin.**
- Make a step by step plan. Never demonstrate an activity for the first time in front of your class without practice.
- Don't spend too long giving explanations. Make your demonstrations short. Have activities ready so pupils can try at least part of the experiment for themselves.

Practical activities in the form of experiments or demonstrations should be an important part of a variety of lessons in subjects across the curriculum. Many can be made with everyday objects. You do not need to have expensive equipment.

In the Primary Science and Social Studies syllabus several topics deal with 'water' (see example below). Topic 48, Project work lists some of these in Science. There are others in Topic 47, Drama, mime and role-play and Topic 44, Using pictures, photographs and diagrams.

Water as a liquid

- As a liquid water takes the shape of whatever container it is placed in.

First, pour water into a bowl, next the same water into an empty bottle and then into a gourd or a tin. Finally, pour it on the ground. The water will spread out and 'disappear' by sinking through the soil.
You can do other experiments with the water and link these to the Project work in Topic 48.

- Floating and sinking
  Pour some water into the plastic bowl. Ask pupils to find a variety of objects (e.g. a small stone, a coin, a leaf, a feather, pieces of paper, or sponge). Drop these into the bowl. Are there some objects that float at first but sink after some time?

- Dissolving
  Do an experiment to show that some substances dissolve in water whilst others do not. Experiment with salt, sugar, coffee powder or tea-leaves, soil, sand or soap powder. Older classes can test if things dissolve more quickly in cold or hot water.

Water as a gas – steam

Boil water in a kettle or a pot. (Let the pupils see the steam rising when the water boils.)

To prove that steam is water in a different state, hold a metal plate over the steam. Water droplets will form on the plate.

Water as a solid – ice

Show pupils that ice is solid. Drop it on a hard surface. It will sound solid and may even break into pieces.

Prove that the ice is water by allowing it to melt.

Topic: The three different states of water

Equipment

A bowl, an empty plastic bottle with the top cut off (e.g.1 litre oil bottle), a variety of containers of different shapes, e.g. gourds or tins, a coal pot, a kettle or pot, and a flat piece of metal (a metal plate).

More examples in other subject areas

Environment Studies	Experiments/Demonstrations
Health	A demonstration showing how to make ORT (Oral Rehydration Therapy) for persons with severe diarrhoea. Use the water filter shown in Topic 11, Making your classroom interesting to work in, to produce clean water.
Mathematics Use children's games to demonstrate probability	In Ghana, girls play a game call *ampe*. Two girls face each other. Both jump in the air and clap their hands. As they land, one foot has to be extended in front of the other. One girl scores if they both extend the same foot, the other if they extend different feet. Jump five times. Who won the game? Now repeat the game 20, 50 and then 100 times. (Record the scores.) What is the probability they will extend the same foot? Who actually wins the most times?
Arts and Crafts Use art or craft ideas in Science and Maths lessons.	Pattern making/printing: Try block printing on material, paper or card. Use leaves, buttons, string or rope even small pieces of bamboo dipped in colour and pressed on to a card.
Use local dyes. (See Using the local area, Topic 58.)	Thread coloured seeds to show recurring patterns. (How many different patterns can you make using twelve seeds of two, three or four different colours?). Fill eight similar glass bottles with different levels of water. When tapped with a stick they will produce different notes. Pupils can make their own instrument by experimenting with different levels of water. They can learn to play tunes.

Once you learn to use experiments and demonstrations with confidence in Science, start to make a list of other areas of the curriculum where they may be appropriate.

42 Using stories in lessons

Example of specific kinds of story

Traditional folk stories, myths and legends

Brer Rabbit (American)
(Find out if your area has similar stories, for example about Kalulu the rabbit.)

Ananse Stories

General stories

Adventure, family and so on.

African history and Africa today

Ancient Kingdoms in Africa

The Slave Trade

Famous African men and women, e.g. Nelson Mandela, Kofi Annan, Mansa Musa, Chaka Zulu, Yaa Asantewa.

Stories with themes, e.g. health, the environment, moral issues

Life in the deserts, forests or coastal areas

Tourism

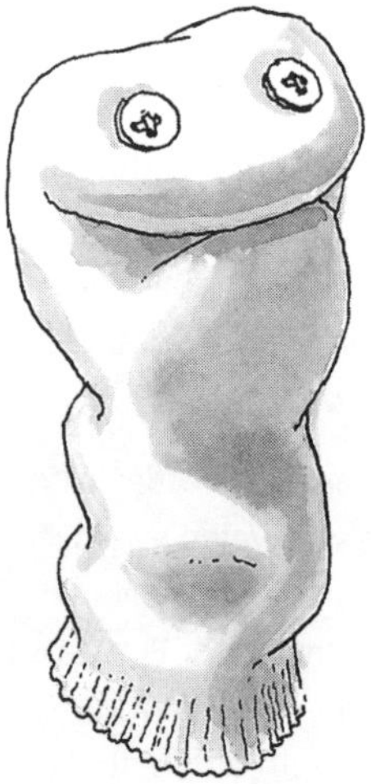

Stories provide a wealth of material that can be used in different ways in different subjects. Across Africa there is a great story-telling tradition. Make use of it as much as you can. Try to gain the interest of your pupils with a story linked to a new topic that you are going to teach.

Make a list of the stories that you know and think about ways these could be used in different lessons. If you have been posted to a region far from your home-town you may not know the local stories. Enlist the help of teachers from the area, older member of the community or some of the older children.

The suggestions made in this section are only a beginning. Stories vary from country to country, and there will be many more from your area. Some African stories are familiar in other countries; the Brer Rabbit stories originated in Africa, for example. See if you can find stories written by local writers and work with parents or the community to build a library in your school.

Telling stories to children

Most pupils enjoy listening to a story. You might be able to invite a parent to help with this activity. (See Involving parents in school activities, Topic 68.) If you have a radio you may be able to listen with your class to children's story-time. There may be stories available on cassettes, or you could record a local story-teller. Let your class sit informally in a circle on the floor in the same way that they might listen to stories around a fire in the evenings.

- When you read or tell stories to your class, try to make it a dramatic, larger than life experience.
- Choose your story carefully. Get to know it well. It should be suitable for all pupils in class.
- Can you find a story (or make one up) that fits in with something you are learning about in class?
- Use props, as actors do. Puppets can be helpful, especially if you are telling a story, rather than reading it. Finger or hand puppets can be made from waste materials, like old socks, with buttons sewn on for eyes.
- A simple musical instrument, like a recorder or drum, can be used to signal a special part of a story.
- Use your voice as an instrument. Vary your tone and use different voices for each character. Make background noises like the wind blowing.
- Pause before the climax of the story. Try to draw the listeners along with you.
- Involve the children in the story by asking questions occasionally. Involve one or two as characters if the story is suitable.

Activity *A story game*

Longer and longer sentences

This game can be played in pairs or in a group. It will help pupils think of descriptive words and phrases that add detail to their writing. The first person begins by writing a simple sentence. Each person then adds or changes one word to make a new sentence.

The woman walked along the road.

The **old** woman walked along the road.

The old woman walked **slowly** along the road.

How long can you make the sentence?

Activity *Ideas for stories*

Work with your pupils to make a list of different types of stories:

- Adventure stories
- School stories
- Animal stories
- Stories about a festival or a celebration
- Real-life stories

Put each type of story on the middle of a 'web' and let pupils think of different ideas they might write about.

- Be aware – are the listeners losing interest and beginning to fidget? Think: **Have I gone on too long? Is the story becoming confused? Is it too difficult?**
- Children love stories that make them laugh. Try to engage their other emotions as well.

Children writing and telling stories

Developing story-telling and writing skills is an important part of language development as it requires children to use their imagination and to use words in an interesting way. Start by getting pupils to play games with words. Topic 43, Poetry, rhymes, songs and riddles gives more ideas for developing imagination and writing skills.

If there are not many books in your school encourage pupils from more senior classes to illustrate and write simple stories for younger groups. Each page should contain one drawing and one or two simple sentences underneath.

- Discuss story ideas that would appeal to younger readers.
- Help pupils to make a list of words that they should be able to read.
- The illustrations are an important part of a story. Remember, they often help young readers to guess the word.

43 Poetry, rhymes, songs and riddles

Activity *Collecting local rhymes and poetry*

A well-known counting rhyme in English is:

One, two tie up my shoe,
Three, four knock at the door,
Five, six pick up sticks,
Seven, eight lay them straight,
Nine, ten a big fat hen.

Work with other teachers, parents and older members of the community to make a collection of poems or rhymes in your local language/s that could be used in your lessons. Try to list them according to the subject, e.g. counting rhymes; poems about the environment or events in the history of your country.

WATER

W arm and wet
A river flowing through the forest
T rees and grasses grow along the banks
E lephants and antelopes drink there in the evening
R eaching the sea

Poetry grew out of an oral tradition of stories, songs and chants. Young children in particular like to repeat sounds, words and phrases. Nursery rhymes, songs and riddles are the first poems that they learn. One of the reasons why teachers find it difficult to teach poetry is because there are very few books available. Many people cannot remember the stories and rhymes they heard as children. This topic outlines some simple ideas that use poetry and rhymes in different subjects.

Using poems in lessons

First read or recite a poem to your pupils so that they can think about its meaning and the way it is written.

- What is the poem about?
- What did they like or dislike about the poem?
- Can they find pattern sounds or the rhythm of the words? Try beating different rhythms on a drum or the top of your desk and ask pupils to make sentences that repeat the rhythm.

Once pupils begin to listen to poetry and to understand the way it is written they can begin to make up their own poems.

Poetry themes

Most poetry has a theme. If you provide some ideas you will find your pupils will enjoy writing about things they like doing or things they see around them. You might also ask pupils to write a short poem like *The Spider* or *Water*, on something they are studying in another subject.

The Spider

The spider made its web across the path
I pushed my finger through the web
The spider ran out to see if it was something good to eat.

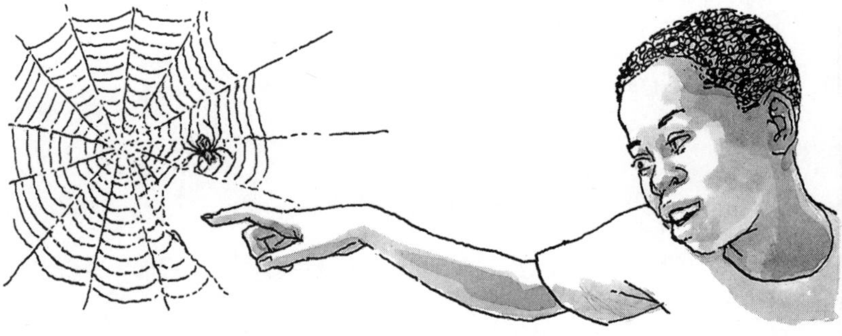

Activity

Ask pupils to write acrostic poems using:

AFRICA, LION or FOREST

or a similar poem using the letters of their name or a word in their own language.

Acrostics

This type of theme poetry is based on the initial letters of a word. Each line of the poem begins with a letter of the word chosen and relates to the meaning of the word, The poem on **WATER** shows how this is done. Is there a similar kind of poetry in your local language?

Riddles

Textbooks sometimes use word guessing games that also explain the meaning of the words. These are riddles. They can help pupils memorise or learn new words associated with a particular theme, e.g. in Social Studies, in a lesson about different ways to travel your pupils might have suggested: train, canoe, donkey, aeroplane.

Riddles

'I go from town to town following an iron road' What am I? (a train)

'Once I lived in the forest now I ride across the waves.' What am I? (a canoe)

Rhymes

Rhyming words help pupils to develop language skills. Some words rhyme because they have similar sounds **e.g. sand**, **band** and **land** or **hot**, **shot** and **spot.** You can use this idea to produce a large number of new rhyming words. Pupils can add one or sometimes two letters to the beginning of the sequence: Try using: **-art -ash -ick** and **-ump**.

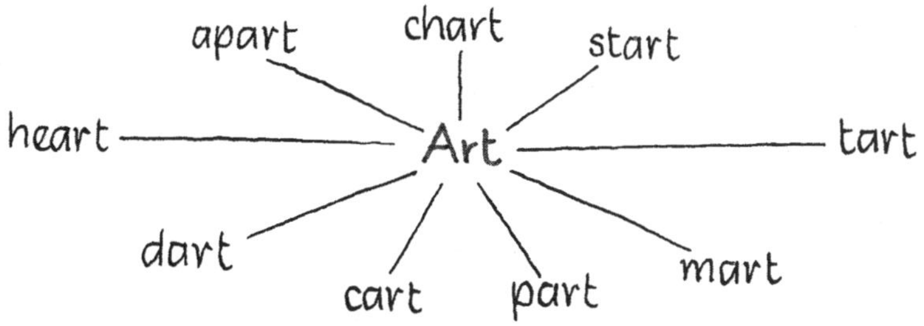

Activity *How many words?*

Going through the alphabet, ask pupils to make up short sentences of three or more words beginning with the same letter.

e.g. **A**ngry **a**nts **a**te **a**n **a**vocado.

Mariama **m**anaged to **m**ake **m**any **m**istakes in **M**aths.

Who can make the longest sentence?

Alliteration

Sometimes rhymes are made by repeating the first sound of a letter: This known as 'Alliteration' A*mazing* a*ntelopes:* b*eautiful* b*ubbles:* c*olourful* c*akes.* The activity box shows how to use this idea.

Songs

Songs can also be used to extend language skills. Many traditional songs tell a story or make a comment about life. Can you think of any in your local language? Can the story be translated into English?

44 Using pictures and diagrams

Pictures, diagrams and photographs can be used to introduce a new topic (e.g. forests or deserts, a hospital, or people from other lands), to provide ideas for vocabulary work, as the theme for story writing or to set the scene for a drama activity. If you do not have a supply of useful pictures learn to draw simple sketches on the board. It is not difficult to learn to draw a variety of stick people.

Descriptions from pictures

Use pictures from your textbooks, or interesting pictures from old calendars or magazines. Give one picture to each group and ask a pupil to describe the scene or ask **What happens next?**

In Social Studies, Science and English pictures and photographs can be used to stimulate pupils to look for the information. Who? What? Where? Doing what? How? When? What's in the foreground, centre, background? What is the picture/photo trying to say, show?

Pictures from descriptions: improving listening skills and imagination

Reversing this procedure is also a good exercise especially where there are not enough books for everyone to use.

- Find an interesting description in a story, read it to the class and then ask them to draw a picture from your description.
- Choose a picture. Do not show it to the class. Describe the scene to them in just four sentences. Let pupils draw a picture from your description. As pupils become more skilled you can add more detail. At the end of the lesson display the picture so that pupils can compare their ideas with your picture. Example: Description: A path goes through the forest. Two women are walking along the path, one is carrying a basket on her head. Extra details can be added, e.g. the two women are old, one is using a stick. The other is carrying a basket of pineapples on her head.

Picture stories

These are very useful for building up story-telling skills.

- **What happened next?** pictures will stimulate ideas for an ending to the story.

- Pupils can draw their own **what happened next?** strips. This can be done in pairs or groups. (See Group work, Topic 33 and Working in pairs, Topic 34.)
- Each picture should be captioned, giving the storyline.
- Speech bubbles and other labels can be added to express other ideas.
- Display the pupils' stories.

Using diagrams

Everyone remembers things more easily if they have a picture in their mind. Topics from Environment Studies or Science can be developed by using diagrams. Use stick people so that the diagrams are easy to draw and have clear labels. Keep the activities simple so that the pupils learn to explain diagrams in their own words.

Flow diagrams

These are similar to **web diagrams** (see Topic 43, Using stories in lessons) in that they help to develop ideas on a particular topic but unlike webs they develop thinking in a particular sequence. They can be used to sequence ideas for a composition – showing ideas for the beginning, the middle and the end – or to structure thinking in an experiment.

45 Using games to improve learning

> ### *Activity* Games
>
> Look through your Maths and English textbooks and make a list of games that have been suggested as part of the activities.
>
> In the Maths books you might find:
>
> - Using number lines for addition or subtraction.
> - Number machines.
> - Magic squares.
>
> In the English books you might find:
>
> - Lucky dip (pupils pick a card and then follow the instruction, e.g. name two people who work in a hospital.)
> - Crosswords
>
> Make a list of local games that you can use in your lessons.

The exercises provided in textbooks are to give pupils practice but they are not always very interesting. It is more fun to reinforce learning and give your pupils a chance to practise their skills if some of the activities in your lessons use games to improve learning.

Players need to learn the **rules** and **routines** for each game, to **reason** or **solve** a problem and to **work out** strategies for winning. Pupils with learning difficulties often find it easier to learn new skills if they are presented in the form of a game. Games such as ludo, snakes and ladders, oware or mankale, draughts or dominoes involve quite difficult mathematical calculations, although we rarely think about these during the game. You may know some of these games by other names.

Maths games

The only resources your pupils will need for the following games are a pencil and some paper or a set of cards numbered from 1 to 10. Use the back of cigarette packets to build up your sets and bottle tops, stones, dried beans, etc as counters.

Action games

- Games like **Simon says** can be adapted for Health habits, e.g. Simon says, 'Clean your teeth'.

Games to help memory

Kim's Game

Game can be played either with objects or with number cards. The objects can come from other parts of the curriculum, e.g. tools, (Technology), equipment for cleaning clothes, common plants (Science) and so on.

- Place a number of small objects on a tray. Begin by allowing pupils a short time to look at the objects then, (out of sight) remove one or two and ask which ones have gone.
- You can also cover the objects and ask them to list as many as possible from memory.
- Younger classes can be given 5 to 10 objects, older groups should be able to memorise 15 to 25 objects.

> ### ***Fuzz – Buzz*** *(develops speed and an understanding of number patterns)*
>
> - Certain numbers must be replaced with the word **fuzz**. You may decide that no one is allowed to say multiples of **3**. Pupils would then take turns: – 1 – 2 – **fuzz** – 4 – 5 – **fuzz** – 7 – 8 – **fuzz.**
> - The game can be made more difficult if pupils are not allowed to say two numbers. The second number, e.g. **4** is replaced by the word **buzz.** The sequence would then be: 1 – 2 – **fuzz** (replacing 3) – **buzz** (replacing 4) – 5 – **fuzz** – 7 – **fuzz – buzz** – 10 – 11 – **'fuzz buzz'** (replacing 12. Gradually increase the speed at which you play the game.

Language games

- These can be played anywhere and without much in the way of resources, except something to write on and with.
- An example is **I spy** where pupils have to guess an object from the initial letter.

Hidden words

This game develops vocabulary. Pupils have to find as many different words as they can from a long word, e.g.:

establishment **intermediate** **concentration** **christmas**

Find the number

- Place two sets of number cards face down. The first player turns over two cards. If they are the same numbers he/she can keep the pair; if they are different numbers the cards are turned face down again **in the same position**. The winner is the person with the most pairs. Encourage pupils to make their own game, e.g. **Odds and Evens**: One player, **A** is Odd and the other **B** is Even. Turn over two cards and total them. Player A keeps all odd pairs, player B keeps all the even pairs.

Following directions

This game helps pupils follow directions and to learn the words commonly used in Maths: odd, even, above, below, between, lowest, highest, some, more than, less than, all, first, second, third. You can play it by using your number cards but if you have no resources this game can be played on the chalkboard.

Play this game in groups, with pupils making up their own direction sentences, e.g:

- Put a 6 between 3 and a 4.
- Make a line of 4 number cards that add up to more than 15.
- Make a line of cards with two odd and two even cards.

Word Chains

WAS	BEAT
GAS	BE**L**T
GA**P**	**M**ELT
TAP	ME**A**T
T**O**P	MEA**L**

The simplest version of this game is to write a word at the top of the board, e.g. **WAS**. Pupils then take it in turns to change **one letter** of that word to form a new word. This can be a group game with a reward for the group with the longest chain. Three or four letter words are easiest to begin with. How many turns will it take to change the word **BLACK** into **WHITE?**

Twenty questions

This game helps players to learn how to ask useful questions and to make use of the answers given to them in order to solve a problem. Two or three children choose an object, e.g. a bicycle. The class is then allowed to ask the team **twenty questions** that will help them find out what the object is. To score they must guess the object before they have used up their twenty questions, e.g: What is the object made from? Is it in the classroom or outside?

Science games

Always try to make Science lessons as active as possible. You will find that some concepts can be taught more effectively through games, for example the movement of the sun or shadows.

- Let one pupil stand on a particular spot. The rest of the group makes an outline of the shadow at different times of the day.
- Play shadow-tag. Outline an area about six paces square. Ten children stand in the square, one is chosen as the 'catcher'. When he/she steps on someone's shadow that child must stand still. The last child to be caught becomes the 'catcher'.
- Make strange animal shapes by combining their shadows (e.g. an octopus – four children kneel close together and wave their eight arms out around the 'body').

Teach pupils to be observant: Ask them to make science observations on their way to school and play **I SPY** or **BINGO**.

I spied some corn growing – it was almost ready to harvest.
I spied – some frogs crossing the road.
I spied – some lizard's eggs.

If you are teaching a particular topic ask pupils to make a BINGO sheet in their exercise book and cross off each item as they see it. Leave enough space for pupils to make a small drawing. If you choose things that can be seen in the school compound your pupils should be able to show you where they saw them.

A bird's nest	A crow	A caterpillar	A spider's web
A termite's nest	A tree frog	A butterfly	A cockroach

46 Puzzles

A crossword puzzle

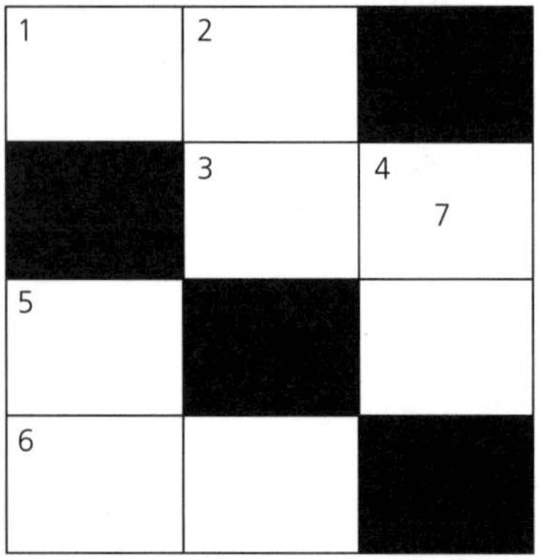

Clues

Across

1 Half of 4 down *(35)*

3 A number that can be divided by 3 *(57)*

6 (2 x 12) or (3 x 8) (4 × 6) *(24)*

Down

2 A multiple of 11 *(55)*

4 10 x 7 *(70)*

5 How many in a dozen? *(12)*

Puzzles can be used to help pupils develop problem-solving skills. Start by giving simple puzzles that are fairly easy to solve, for example, jigsaws for younger pupils. If the puzzle is too difficult pupils may give up.

- Explain what pupils have to find out. They will need time to solve the puzzle by themselves. If anyone can solve the problem, see if he/she can explain how they did it.
- After everyone has had a chance to complete the puzzle go through the steps with the class and then put a similar puzzle on the board so that everyone can try again. This section gives examples of several different types of puzzle.

Crossword puzzles

- There are usually simple crossword puzzles in the English textbook or in your local newspaper on the Children's page. Let pupils practise these first (the answers are usually given on the following day). You can find more difficult puzzles later. You will need to solve the first crossword with pupils as they may not understand the way that clues are given.
- You may also like to use Number Crosswords

Remind pupils to look for answers they are sure of – to fill them in and that will give them a clue for one or two more answers. In this example:

Find the answer to 4 Down first (10 x 7 = 70) – that will help to answer to 1 Across. There will then be a clue (the 5) that will help to answer 2 Down. Two figure multiples of eleven always repeat the same number, e.g.22 or 33. The answer to 2 down must therefore be 55. If that is filled in they will have found the correct answer for 3 across. Finally work out 6 across and 5 down.

- Science, Social Studies or Religious Knowledge can provide good words for crosswords or wordsearches. Pupils can work in pairs to make up a word puzzle. Another pair can solve it.

Wordsearch puzzles

Hidden in the box on the next page you will find seven trees commonly found in Africa.

Teak, Mahogany, Ebony, Nim, Rubber,

Palm, Acacia

The wordsearch

K	A	T	E	E	M	R	M
P	O	N	N	M	P	I	E
A	T	E	B	O	N	Y	H
L	E	O	A	G	U	R	R
M	A	H	O	G	A	N	Y
I	K	Y	B	E	E	T	O
G	A	C	A	C	I	A	N
R	E	B	B	U	R	C	A
K	E	M	C	P	A	L	I
B	P	L	I	T	E	U	L

List words to find in wordsearch below.

Teak, Mahogany, Ebony, Nim, Rubber, Palm, Acacia

- In wordsearch puzzles pupils look for words hidden among the letters filling a square. You may find examples of wordsearches in your local paper. The letters must be in the correct sequence but may be written in a horizontal or vertical direction or on a diagonal. They may be written from right to left or backwards.
- Show pupils how to solve the puzzle systematically.

1 Look along all the horizontal rows from right to left and then from left to right. (They should find **EBONY, ACACIA, RUBBER** and **MAHOGANY.)**

2 Look at the columns from top to bottom and then from bottom to top. (They should find **TEAK** and **PALM.**

3 Finally work along each row in a diagonal direction. They should then find **NIM.**

Code puzzles

Most pupils like writing coded messages to each other. These may substitute numbers for letters, letters for letters or letters for numbers.

- Here is the most simple code:

A	B	C	D	E	F	G	H
1	2	3	4	5	6	7	8

- Try starting the code in a different place in the alphabet.
- You may find some examples of coded puzzles in your Maths textbook, like these:

```
C D E          K K 8
2 2 1 +        1 7 K  _    Which clues help solve
______         _____       these problems?
E 9 D          3 8 3
______         _____
```

- Make up some codes of your own.

Other puzzles

- Jigsaws can be made from pictures of all sorts. Try cutting photographs, maps, poems, pictures of machinery, etc. into irregular pieces for others to reassemble. The puzzle can be made longer lasting by sticking it to a piece of card before you begin cutting.
- Treasure maps are always fun to make and follow. One group of pupils could make a Maths trail around the classroom or a nature trail around the compound with a map for another group to follow.

47 Drama, mime and role-play

Definitions

Drama An activity where the actors use words written by someone else. African playwrights include Wole Soyinka or Ama Ata Aidoo.

Improvisation A short drama/play where the players make up the words and actions. The performances are rarely written down and the players improvise/make up the words as the story progresses. Useful for exploring motivation and interaction in Social Studies, e.g. peer pressure.

Role-play Children enjoy games involving role-play (pretending to be someone else) from a very early age, e.g. use activities involving a shop in lessons to help pupils understand sums dealing with money. Role-play can also be linked to other lessons as it helps pupils learn about people and situations that they may not necessarily have experienced.

Mime Acting without words, the idea is conveyed through actions. It can be used in situations where pupils have a limited vocabulary, or where you want to give pupils an opportunity to develop a character or an idea without words or for guessing games.

There is a long tradition of community dance and drama in Africa and in many countries there are groups of actors and musicians who go from village to village performing plays. Schools often perform short plays during morning assembly or to mark important traditional or religious ceremonies. Many teachers use drama, mime or role-play during regular class work. This is a valuable technique that can provide pupils with opportunities not only to examine both real-life and imaginary situations but also to explore their own ideas, attitudes and feelings.

Planning activities

Successful activities need very few resources: a space and time to play and perhaps a box containing a variety of materials and objects to stimulate their imagination. Collect a selection of different pieces of cloth, these are more useful than dresses or shirts as they can be used in many different ways, e.g. as cloaks, head-dresses or costumes. Parents or friends might also provide a selection of small objects such as keys or foreign coins and clean empty tins, containers or empty boxes of food products.

Real-life situations

Begin by allowing pupils to develop a role-play on familiar topics relating to their lives, shopping in the market, getting ready for school or buying new clothes. Some ideas, such as a visit to the hospital could become the focus of a whole class role-play. The teacher might assign roles: the doctor, nurses, patients and visitors. The pupils could suggest situations. Follow-up activities could include vocabulary work, story writing and topics on basic health.

Developing questioning skills through role-play (for older pupils)

Work in pairs/ interviewing: one person is the interviewer the other the character:

- What questions would you ask a radio or TV newsreader in order to find out about their job?
- Giving accurate directions: one person is the robot, the other gives directions. Guide your robot through a series of obstacles (under a table, over a chair, through the door).

> ### *Activity* Using drama, mime and role-play across the curriculum
>
> The list identifies a number of skills that primary pupils are expected to develop.
>
> **Pupils should be able to:**
> - Listen and understand.
> - Give directions or messages.
> - Question and answer.
> - Give clear descriptions of observations and experiences.
> - Understand sequencing.
> - Interpret information.
> - Predict what will happen.
>
> Make a list of drama, mime or role-play activities in different subjects that would help to develop these skills.

Think about feelings and reactions

You will need to provide an opportunity for pupils to explore ideas and feelings. Discuss issues such as prejudice, bullying, stealing, or cruelty, through characters and drama. One technique is to put the person/s playing the role in the centre of a circle. At the end of the scene, members of the class are allowed to question the person/s playing the role. They must answer the questions in the role they are playing. Allow pupils to explore social roles in the community, e.g. a traditional ruler, an elder, a district official.

Mime

Mime can help to develop skills of observation and interpretation. Ask pupils to mime:

- **Characters**: a goalkeeper; a robot; a clown or a traffic policeman.
- **Verbs** to use instead of **said :** shouted, whispered, screamed, grumbled.
- **Words** that show: **movement**: bouncing, crawling, dancing, floating.
- **Actions** or **Situations:**

  1 Walk like a person with a stiff leg, or someone carrying a very heavy object.

  2 Listen like a person who cannot hear very well.

  3 Cut down a large tree, cut grass, cut a piece of paper.

- **Bring out differences** in the meaning of words: **Search** for a small object in the grass; **look** for a friend in a crowd. **Clean** the car; **wash** a baby's face or **scrub** clothes.
- **Show** how you feel: angry, sad, happy, bored, guilty, hungry.

48 Project work

Activity *Introducing a project*

Look at the **Water Project** and make a list of the topics that you could develop with your year group.

You might also talk to a teacher in another year group (or on the afternoon shift) and see if you could work on the project together. (See Topic 66, Working with other staff.)

Project work is time-consuming but by linking topics in a common theme, interest is stimulated and learning encouraged across several curriculum subjects.

Choosing a topic

Many interesting topics such as water, air, shapes, numbers, metals, clothes, plants, animals, homes, transport can be linked across several subjects and developed as class or school projects. Choose a topic that is relevant to work being done during the term and brainstorm ideas with other teachers in your school or year group. Once you have the main ideas, you can plan graded activities that provide work for children of different abilities or age groups.

The web diagram on the next page looks at a project on the theme of **Water**. Some suggestions are obviously part of the curriculum for older pupils, others are more suitable for younger pupils.

Introducing a water project to your class

You need to capture the interest of your pupils right from the start. Here are three different ways you might introduce the topic of **Water**.

- Ask pupils to find or draw pictures that show water in some way. Their pictures will probably show a variety of ideas that you can develop: a running tap, a river or lake, a rainy day.
- Ask pupils to look around the school compound/their homes and to list the different ways water is obtained and used. These may include water from taps, stand-pipes, ponds or wells. The water may be used for gardening, cooking, washing, or toilets. Develop a discussion on water **conservation**.
- Read a story about water, e.g. Noah's Ark or building a great dam.

Activity *Discussion*

Develop a whole class discussion (or a discussion between two classes) on water. Every child will have experienced periods of water shortage or the floods that result from prolonged heavy rain. Ask them to talk about its effects on their family, on farms or on life in the town. Most will also be aware of diseases that are linked to water.

Group and individual work

Provides an opportunity for pupils to work individually on a project or to choose their own group. You may decide to provide a variety of activities that all groups have to complete or separate activities that can be linked together later. Make sure that each activity has clear, simple instructions. These should be written on firm card (from empty boxes) as several groups may use each activity.

Displays of project work

Gradually build up a display of your pupils' work. Discuss with pupils how the material may be presented. (See Displaying pupil's work, Topic 55.) Encourage groups to make their displays interesting to look at with pictures, drawings, models and collections. Do not ask for too much written work. Try to arrange the display in time for an Open Day at school. This can give an opportunity for each group to explain to interested parents or pupils from other classes about their part in the project.

Project plan

Discussion topics

The water cycle, rain, condensation, evaporation.
Rivers, lakes and seas
The effect of floods and drought on farming and communities
Water conservation

Language

Vocabulary: words to describe water: stream, flow, splash, drip
'Watery activities': swimming, water-skiing, diving, sailing
Stories: 'Jonah and the Whale' or 'Noah's Ark'
Traditional poems or stories about river or sea monsters or Gods

Maths

Liquid measurement: litres, gallons
Capacity: full, empty,
Volume: filling containers
Displacement, speed and flow

Environment studies

Water and weather: rainfall, snow, hail, mist, clouds
Water and health: River blindness, malaria, cholera
Water pollution
Jobs associated with water: work in a port, fishing, underwater exploration

Project topic

Water

Science

Water as a liquid, a solid or a gas: freezing, thawing, heating
Floating and sinking
Reflections, ripples, waves and bubbles
Water and growing plants
Animals that live in water

Art work

Find pictures showing water scenes
Patterns of wavy lines: drag a comb across wet paint
'Stippling': wet the surface of a piece of paper and then drop small spots of paint or coloured ink on the wet paper
Tie and dye

Technology

Water power: hydro electric power (HEP), water wheels
Cooking: boiling, steaming
Food processing: drying, soaking, dissolving, diluting
Cooling water without a fridge

Music/Drama

'The Lost Fisherman'
Songs about the sea
Fill glass bottles with different levels of water and listen to the sound when tapped with a stick. Arrange them in sequence from lowest to highest and learn to play a tune.

49 Assessing your resources

> ***Activity*** *What resources are available to your school?*
>
> *Where are they located?*
>
> Use this as a guide. Make your own chart, or one for the school with the help of other teachers. Add any other resources that you have found useful.

Resources
reference books
magazines/newspapers
science kits
maps or a globe
class sets of reading books
collections of pictures
worksheets
models
scissors
glue or sellotape
coloured pens/pencils

> ***Activity*** *Using junk materials*
>
> - Ask pupils to collect junk materials such as empty tins or cardboard boxes.
> - See who can build the most imaginative model.

Resources available in your school

If you want to improve the quality of your activities and lessons you need to know exactly what resources are available and where you can find them. If you make a careful survey you may well find that your resources are not as limited as you first thought. The first activity will help you find out what there is in the school. Some material may be very old or spoiled. Check with other teachers or the head teacher first and then throw it away. Start collecting new material. (See Collecting and storing resources, Topic 50.) Keep a list of what everyone has so that you can all use the resources co-operatively. The resources should be checked every time they are used to make sure they are in good order.

What other resources can you use?

Very often we think of resources as materials such as apparatus, maps and charts or science kits that need to be bought by your school. There are however many other resources both material and human that could be used which do not need to be bought. Topic 57, Using the school compound will give you some ideas.

Human resources – people in your village or town

Other ways of involving members of the community are detailed in Topic 58. Keep a list of people who could help you in school.

- Parents or local people who could be invited to talk about their work or who might be willing to allow pupils to visit their place of work.
- Older people who remember historical events.
- Craftsmen and women.
- Men and women who know about the local area and environment.

(Look at Topic 68, Involving parents in school activities.)

Ways of using free resources

Primary teachers seldom throw anything away. This is a wise thing to do – what someone else may call junk is often perfect for making a model.

- Save wire to make vehicles or furniture.
- Scraps of material can be turned into cloth dolls or animals.
- Wood can be used for model cars, go-carts (with wheels saved from something else), furniture.
- Cardboard boxes and rolls make wonderful modelling material.

Plant	Part used	Method	Colour obtained
Avocado pear	Seeds	Grind seeds; mix with a little water, stand and strain.	Brown
Cola	Nuts	As above	Reddish-brown
Onions	Dried skin	Soak or boil the skins. Stand for some time, strain and use liquid.	Yellow-brown
Sorghum	Dried leaves and stems	Pound leaves and stems – soak in water, stand and strain.	Dark red
Teak tree	Young leaves	Crush and pound leaves – mix with water, stand and strain.	Bright red
Mango tree	Bark	Crush and pound dried bark – mix with water, stand and strain.	Yellow
Ash	Wood/charcoal	Mix with water, add salt, stir and leave to settle.	Yellow-brown

Local plants

You may want to do some art and craft work with your pupils as part of a lesson or as a follow up to a visit from a craftsperson.

- Dyes are expensive to buy but there are a number of plants in your area that can be processed to make dyes.
- The chart will give you some ideas about using dyes.

Getting access to those resources that are not in your own classroom.

- Is there a list of all the resources in your school?
- Is there a special place (a room, cupboard or boxes) to store resources?
- Is there someone who is responsible for keeping a record of resources and allocating them to teachers who need them?

If you have answered 'No' to any of these questions you will need to find time to list all your resources properly and find somewhere to store them. This is a project that will need the support of your head and other teachers.

50 Collecting and storing resources

Resources are costly to buy but teachers are great collectors and many find very imaginative ways to recycle material and to make use of scraps. Encourage your pupils to collect materials that will be useful in lessons.

Useful items to collect

The resources listed below should be available in most areas.

newspapers

photographs and birthday or greetings cards

scraps of different types of material

stamps

coloured plastic bags

cardboard boxes or cartons of different sizes and shapes

plastic containers or 'squeezy' bottles

empty jars, bottles and tins of various sizes

shells

string, rope and rubber bands

short pieces of hose pipe

foam sponges

seeds/beans

gourds and bamboo

bottle tops

small pieces of wood that can be cut into squares, circles, triangles or rectangles

a mirror

You may also find some of these items.

pictures from old magazines/calendars

posters from the local museum or tourist board

egg trays

corks

foil paper

cotton reels

wire coat hangers

inner tubes from toilet paper

Activity *Using your collections*

It is all too easy to make collections and then rarely use them. Collections of stones, empty nests, leaves, plants or bones, for example, may be displayed on a Science table for many months and yet not be part of any of the lessons being taught. After a while nobody bothers to look at the material. Use ideas from the topic on display. (Displaying pupils' work, Topic 55.) Use a chair or a desk top to show objects that reflect the topics that you are teaching and change the collection each week.

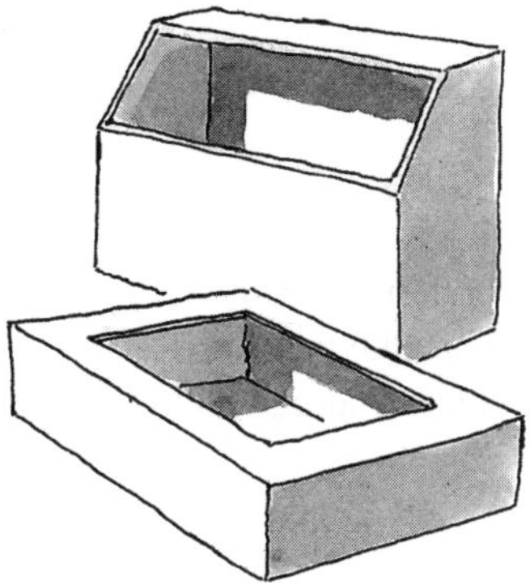

Keep a list of how your collections can be used

Collections	Use in lessons
Square cards from cigarette boxes, sugar cube cartons or boxes	Maths: area, perimeter, four-sided figures/right angles. Flash cards in English or other subjects.
Measuring tins, plastic bottles, bowls, buckets	Volume capacity, Science experiments.
Bundles of sticks (each child should collect twelve of the same size)	Number placement; congruent lines; exploring enclosed shapes, (3/4 or more sides), angles; perimeter, area.
Stones, bottle tops, seeds	Sets; number placement; graphs, Maths vocabulary **more than, less than**, **larger than**, etc.
Dice (usually available as many people play ludo)	Counting games, probability.
Lengths of string, **pegs and hangers**	Making a circle; measurement, displaying pupils' work, making mobiles.
Floor mats	Make group and drama work easier. Can be used as a background for displays.

Keeping track of and storing resources

If they are to be used effectively, you will need to store and label your resources properly.

If there are no cupboards or shelves, empty cartons from a local shop can also be used to store materials.

When they are not in use, keep your resources in boxes that are clearly labelled. Display a list of all the resources you have collected and the name or number of the box where they are stored. At least once each term find time to sort out your resource materials. Pupils are usually more than willing to help with sorting and labelling. Make an effort to replace material that is no longer useful or in good condition.

51 Taking care of textbooks

> ***Activity*** *Problems with books*
>
> Have a look at the textbooks and exercise books in your class. If they look in poor condition make a note of the main problems.
>
> - Which children are not taking care of their books?
> - Are there any small repairs that you can do with your class?
> - What rewards can you give to pupils who take care of their books?

Textbooks and exercise books are very expensive and hard to replace. Even though you may not have many books in your class you may be very concerned that some children do not take care of them properly. It is important to show your pupils how to protect their books. Here are some guidelines to help you show them how to look after their books properly.

Keeping books clean

Many pupils bring exercise books to school that are torn and dirty. You may like to encourage them to cover their books but in some areas it will be difficult to find suitable materials. There are, however, a number of other ways that you can encourage your pupils to keep their books in good condition.

> **Things they should NEVER do**
>
> - Put books on the ground if it is wet or dirty.
> - Play with books near very small brothers or sisters.
> - Do their homework on a table that has food or drink on it.
> - Leave a book open and face down on a table or desk. It can easily get dirty and eventually the centre binding will break and pages will come loose.

Taking care of books

Very few school books are now printed with a hard cover. Paperbacks are easily damaged by careless handling. Show pupils how to use their books properly.

- Encourage pupils to protect their books from the rain and dirt by keeping them in a plastic bag. Bags made from small 5 kg plastic rice bags are usually available in the local market. You could easily show your pupils how to make them in one of your lessons.
- Students often help with handing out or collecting books. Always insist that the class monitor should hand the book to each child or place it carefully on their desks.
- Show your pupils how to turn the pages by carefully holding the top or bottom corner of the page. Don't let them hold the middle of the page and push the pages over.
- Sometimes pupils cannot remember where they have reached in their book. They should never turn down the corner of the page to remind them of their place. Show them how to make a bookmark from a piece of card or string.

Making simple repairs

The covers of exercise books can be torn very easily. Stick Sellotape along the spine at the front and back and inside the cover. This will strengthen the cover and prevent it from being torn off.

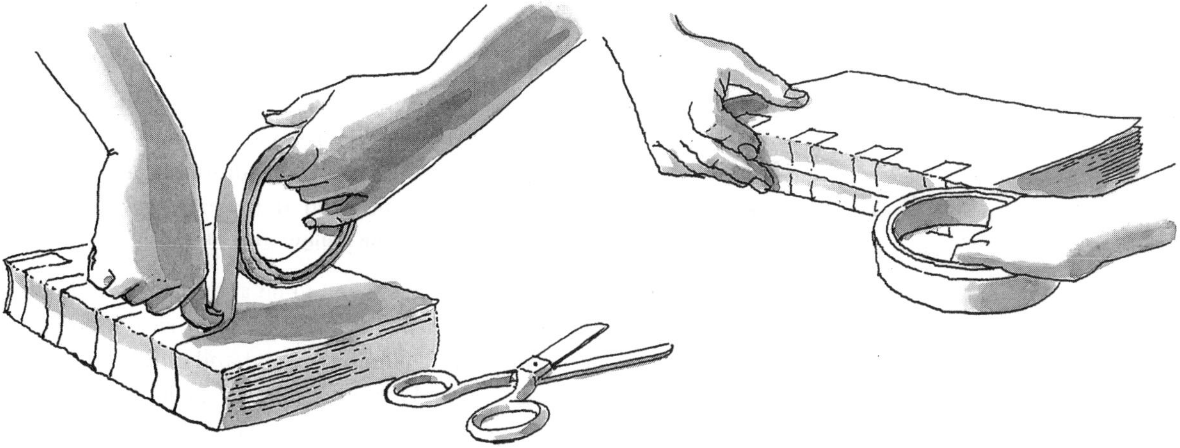

Textbooks in the class

In some schools textbooks and other resource books are kept in the classroom. You may have a cupboard, open shelves or a bookcase that can be used for this purpose. Store textbooks and exercise books in neat piles. If they are not used for some time always make sure they are dusted regularly. Books can also be stored in cartons. If these boxes are grouped together they can provide space for displaying small collections and can easily be moved to a store room for safety either at the end of the day or at the end of each term (see Collecting and storing resources, Topic 50).

52 Teaching aids

> ***Activity** Available teaching and learning materials*
>
> Which of the following teaching and learning aids are available for use in your class?
>
> Which do you use in your lessons?
>
> **Visual materials**
>
> Maps Pictures
>
> Charts Pupil's work
>
> **Practical materials**
>
> Flash cards Activity cards
>
> Work cards
>
> Locally woven mats (as screens, background for displays)
>
> Floor mats (extra seating for group work)
>
> Large pieces of strong material (paper or cloth) suitable for painting (map, picture, etc. for floor work)
>
> Apparatus and models

Teaching aids are an essential part of the learning process. It is important for pupils to have a variety of learning experiences. If teachers provide materials that add interest to the lesson this can help to reinforce learning. In some schools teachers receive a small supply of resource materials from their Ministry of Education or a local NGO, in others they have to make things for themselves. This section looks at a variety of different teaching aids that you, and other teachers in your school, could produce at a relatively low cost.

As you plan your lessons at the beginning of the term, decide what teaching and learning materials would be most useful and how you or your pupils will use them. Work together with other teachers to provide a greater variety of materials that can be shared. Visual aids are used most frequently by teachers but don't forget the value of using local objects, or making models. (See Making simple models and apparatus, Topic 53.)

Producing visual material

The way in which visual aids are presented has an impact on the value of the material as a teaching aid.

Labels and lettering

Use thick dark strokes for letters, words and numbers and make sure that letters are large enough to be read at the back and sides of the class. You can add interest by using coloured felt pens but remember some children are colour blind and cannot tell the difference between red and green or yellow and blue.

Words used for headings or labels, need to be about 2 to 3cm high. You may decide to use a mixture of upper and lower case letters in classes where pupils are just beginning to read and may be unfamiliar with capital letters. Writing of this size needs practice. Draw guide-lines, in pencil, across the page. When the letters are properly spaced and in a straight line you can ink them in and rub out the pencil marks.

Keep it simple

The diagrams giving tips on making teaching aids show two different ways of presenting material. Both sheets give the same information but the one on the left is much easier to read from a distance and will be easier to remember.

PREPARING VISUAL AIDS	Preparing Visual Aids
WRITE CLEARLY	• Writing should be clear.
USE SHORT SIMPLE SENTENCES	• Ideas should be simple and sentences short. Try to limit sentences/points to a single line of six or seven words.
USE PICTURES AND DRAWINGS	• A picture or an object can say quickly and simply what it takes many words to explain.
USE STRONG DARK COLOURS FOR BACKGROUND AND LETTERING	• A dark background colour or lettering makes a better impact because the material stands out clearly.
LIMIT THE AMOUNT OF INFORMATION ON EACH SHEET	• Limit the information on each sheet to one activity with two or three questions to each activity.

Displaying material

Before displaying material check it very carefully for mistakes (in the information or the spelling). Make corrections where necessary.

Provide a background for your material by using large locally woven grass mats, a piece of cloth, fish-net or several plain cardboard sheets (cut from large empty cartons). Sometimes material is put too high for smaller pupils to read easily. You can always vary the level of material by pegging it to clothes hangers or string.

Preparing worksheets

Most schools do not have the facilities to make multiple copies of teaching material. You will need to find ways of making activity sheets that can be easily copied by your pupils.

Pin a numbered series of activity cards around the classroom, on the chalkboard, along the walls or in the middle of a group of desks. Small groups can work at their own pace and copy the information and questions into their notebooks. If the activity cards are numbered you can grade activities to suit a range of age or ability groups, e.g. **The red group should do activities 1 and 2 and the blue group should do activities 3 and 4. If you finish your work quickly try the other activities.**

Activity *Making activity cards and worksheets*

Place on a desk several objects with contrasting qualities, e.g. soft and hard. Put the Activity card near the objects and give each pupil a blank worksheet.

Activity Card 1 Sorting

Look at the objects arranged on the desk.

Draw two circles on your worksheet.

Label one SOFT and the other HARD.

Sort the objects into sets and draw them in the correct circle.

53 Making simple models and apparatus

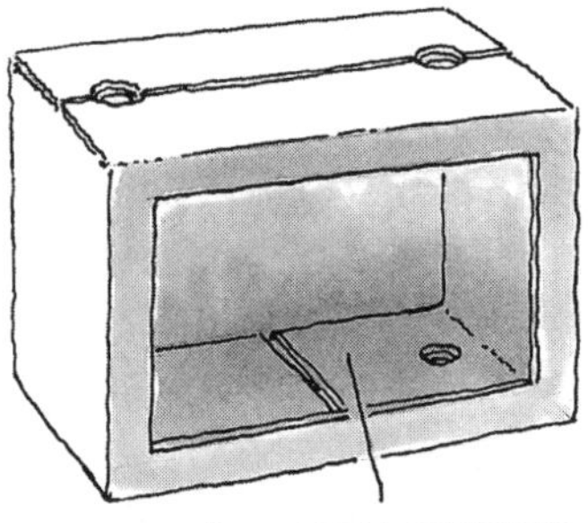

This topic gives suggestions for making three dimensional models and some simple apparatus that can be used in your lessons.

Make your own television

You could use this for number work, spelling patterns or pictures to illustrate a story from history or life in other parts of the world.

Equipment: a cardboard box, two short fairly thick sticks, and a long sheet of paper.

Method: Sellotape together unlined pages from an exercise book to make a long sheet. Information is drawn on the paper and then rolled around the two sticks. The information sheet can be changed according to the lesson.

A diorama

This is simply a scene in a cardboard box.

Cut away one of the long sides of a cardboard box. A scene can be painted on a sheet of paper which is attached to the backdrop. Objects or cut-out figures can also be displayed on the floor of the diorama. You might develop a 3D model of a desert with sand dunes, camels and cactus or a scene showing a local festival.

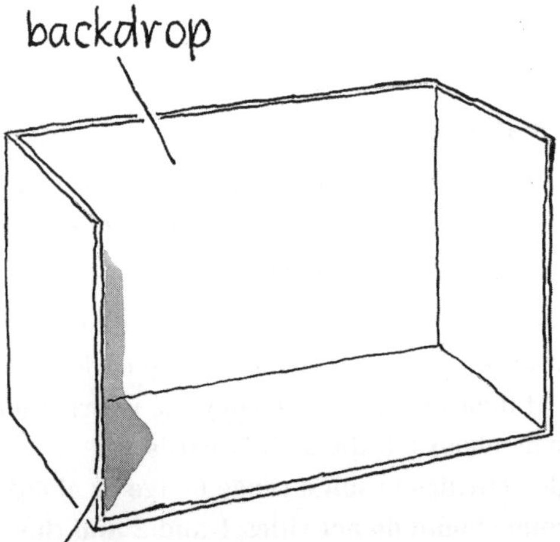

Apparatus

A weather study might use a wind sock to measure the wind direction, or a shadow stick to measure shadows, or a rain gauge to measure rainfall.

A rain gauge

Equipment: a large plastic bottle, a plastic bag, a large and a small circle of wire (from a metal hanger) and string.

Cut the plastic bottle in half and push the top half into the bottom half. Bury it away from buildings and leave about 30 cm of the funnel above ground

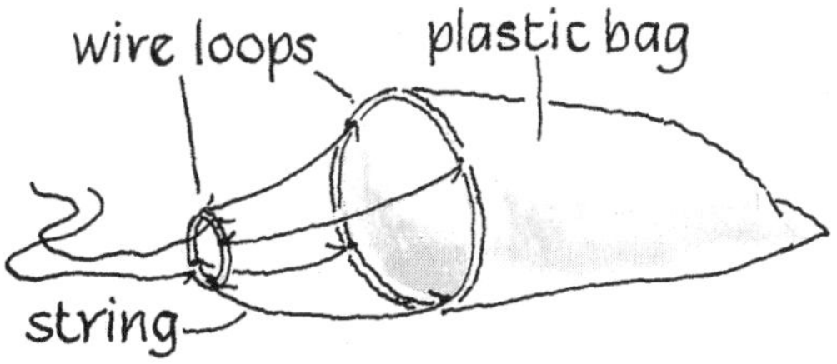

A wind sock

Activity *Using the ideas*

Go through the syllabus topics you are going to teach this year.

How could you use each of these ideas in your lessons?

Wind experiments could also make use of **parachutes, shuttlecocks, windmills or simply a piece of card on a string**

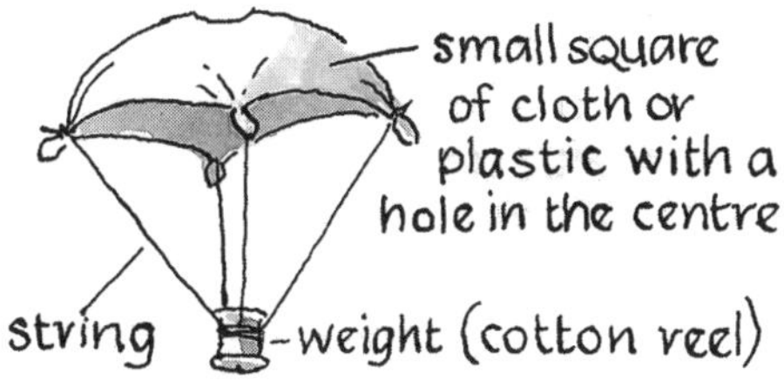

Weighing scales

Equipment: two empty plastic cartons or small (tuna) tins, string, a nail, a wooden frame.

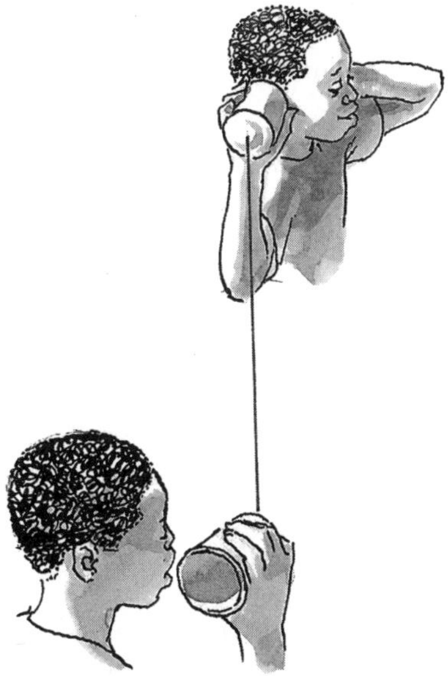

Make a telephone

Equipment: two small plastic cartons or small tins and a long piece of string. Punch a hole in the bottom of each tin; thread the string between the tins. When pupils want to talk on the telephone they should keep the string stretched out.

54 Using the chalkboard

Activity *A diagram of the water cycle*

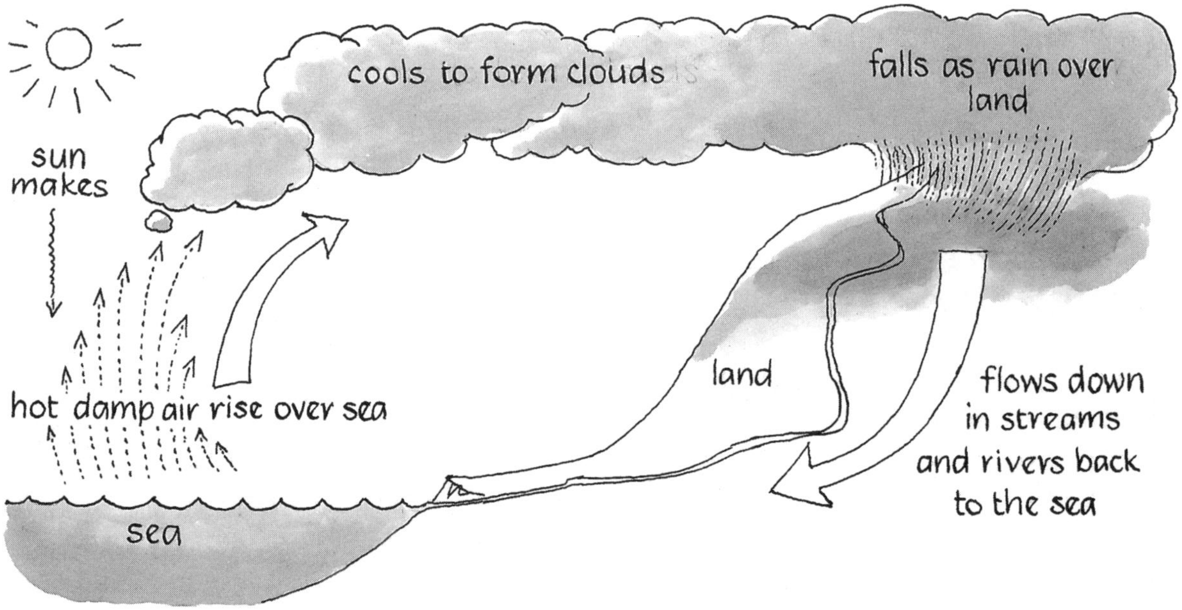

The chalkboard is an invaluable teaching aid and, in some classrooms, it may be the only teaching resource available. Make sure you use it effectively.

Provide key points

- A list of not more than 10 key words or words that are difficult to spell.
- Simple diagrams for pupils to explain or label for themselves. (See Using pictures, photographs and diagrams, Topic 44.)
- One or two clearly worked examples (e.g. of sums).

Talking to the chalkboard

Some teachers give an explanation whilst they are writing on the board. If you are facing the board it is difficult for pupils to hear what is being said and it is not easy for them to ask questions.

- Tell them what you are going to do on the board.
- Ask them to put down their pens and pencils and watch carefully.
- When you have finished writing, turn round, explain what you have done and then give pupils an opportunity to ask questions.

Do not ask pupils to copy work as you are writing

Some pupils will not be able to see what has been written and they will either move around to get a clear view or ask their neighbour.

Make sure that you are standing to the side of the board

If you are right-handed, stand on the left side of the board facing the class. In that way you can see the class and point to the information.

Common mistakes

- **'Chalk and talk'**
  Some teachers cover the board with detailed information. This is **not** the most effective way of teaching.

- **Avoid making detailed notes**
  This actually stops students from thinking and developing their own language skills. It may even result in them paying little or no attention to the lesson as the information is already on the board. Try to build up the learning as you go along. Exercises requiring pupils to fill in the blank are also limited in value.

How often should pupils write on the board?

Not all pupils can write clearly on the board. Their writing may be small and uneven and therefore difficult to read, or the writing speed may be slow. You may, however, feel that it is important to allow pupils to make a contribution to the lesson that is written on the board.

- Ask groups to prepare a few questions relating to the lesson and write these on the board.
- Build up notes on the board with pupils contributing the main points (teacher writes words).
- Ask individuals to fill in the labels on a diagram or map (one or two words).
- Teacher writes pupils' ideas on the board, e.g. in a brainstorm.

Using the board as a teaching aid

To clean or not to clean?

- Opinions differ. Some teachers prefer to start the lesson with a clean surface and to build up information as the lesson proceeds. This allows pupils to discover information for themselves.
- Others like to put an outline of a diagram, key points or a map on the board so they can fill in details as they go along.
- Where schools work a double shift you may have little chance to prepare the board in advance and may have to clean the board at the end of the session.

Check for visibility

- Sometimes sunlight can make it difficult for pupils sitting in certain areas of the classroom to see. It may also be difficult for pupils at the back of the room to see what is written on the bottom half of the board.

Make sure

- Your writing is large and clear.
- Words are spelled correctly.
- Lines are straight.
- Information is well spaced and easy to follow.

This takes practice.

55 Displaying pupils' work

> ***Activity** The importance of display*
>
> Think of four reasons why displays of work play an important part in the pupils' learning.

Many topics within the primary syllabus provide opportunities to develop exciting displays using everyday objects. There are often interesting learning materials on the walls of lower primary classes. Middle and upper primary classrooms need stimulating displays of work just as much as the younger ones. This topic shows **why** displays are important and **how** they can be done without costing too much.

Good reasons for displays of work

- Displays make your classroom look interesting and cared for.
- Special interest displays (such as the Water project. Project work, Topic 48) help pupils understand a topic and the way that it can be linked to several different areas of the curriculum.
- Displays can stimulate questions and a desire to find out more about the topic.
- Displays are a way of showing that you value a good piece of work by your pupils.
- Displays can also be used to show the interests of your pupils.

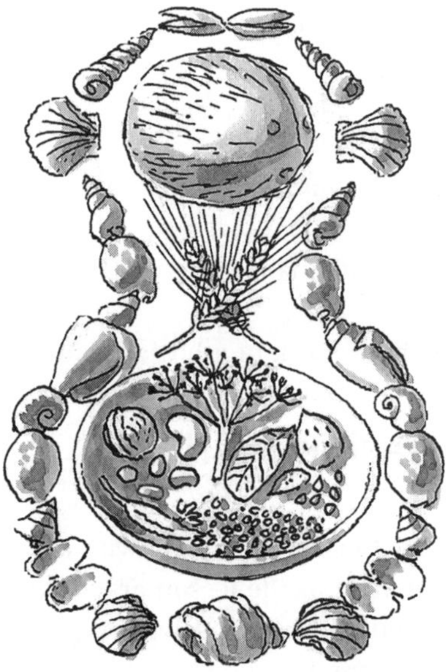

What resources do you need?

Some of the materials suggested here may have been donated, some you may have to borrow.

- **The main display area**: large cardboard cartons, short pieces of pipe, tins and cardboard boxes of various sizes, bricks or cement blocks, unused desks or chairs
- **Background material**: brown cement paper, cloth, fishing nets, palm screens or grass mats
- **Displaying small objects brought in/made by the pupils**: These can be displayed in local woven baskets, gourds, the lids of boxes or tins. Alternatively you can make a loop from thick rope or string and put small objects inside the circle.

What space is available to make a display of work?

If you have a small, overcrowded classroom you may need to use quite a bit of imagination.

- **A wall** is the most obvious area, because it is out of the way and provides a large area of space. The surface may need some preparation before it can be used.
- **Shelves** are also useful. If you do not have any see if a local builder (one of your parents?) will donate a long plank. Stand it on four bricks.
- **Ceilings and the area immediately outside your room** may be useful for small temporary displays.

Preparing walls to hold displays

The walls of many classrooms are made from cement or mud brick and it is not very easy to fix displays of work on them. They will need a framework that can be used to support the display material. You may be able to find a sawmill that produces battens – thin strips of wood about four to six feet long. These can be nailed into the wall and then large pieces of cardboard cut from cartons or woven palm mats fixed across two battens. This type of framework may cost some money and you may need to encourage parents or a local firm to make a contribution. Once in place however, it will last for a long time.

Free-standing displays

You may not always want to pin displays on the classroom wall. For some purposes you may prefer to have a free-standing display. There are a variety of materials that can be used for this kind of display: cardboard boxes, cement blocks or short sections of pipe, a bench, a chair or a desk. This kind of display is best placed in a corner of your room where it is not likely to be knocked over. Try to add variety by making a multi-level display. Some of the boxes you use may have labels or adverts on them that will take attention away from your display. Cover them with a piece of cloth or drape a large piece of fishing net over the side.

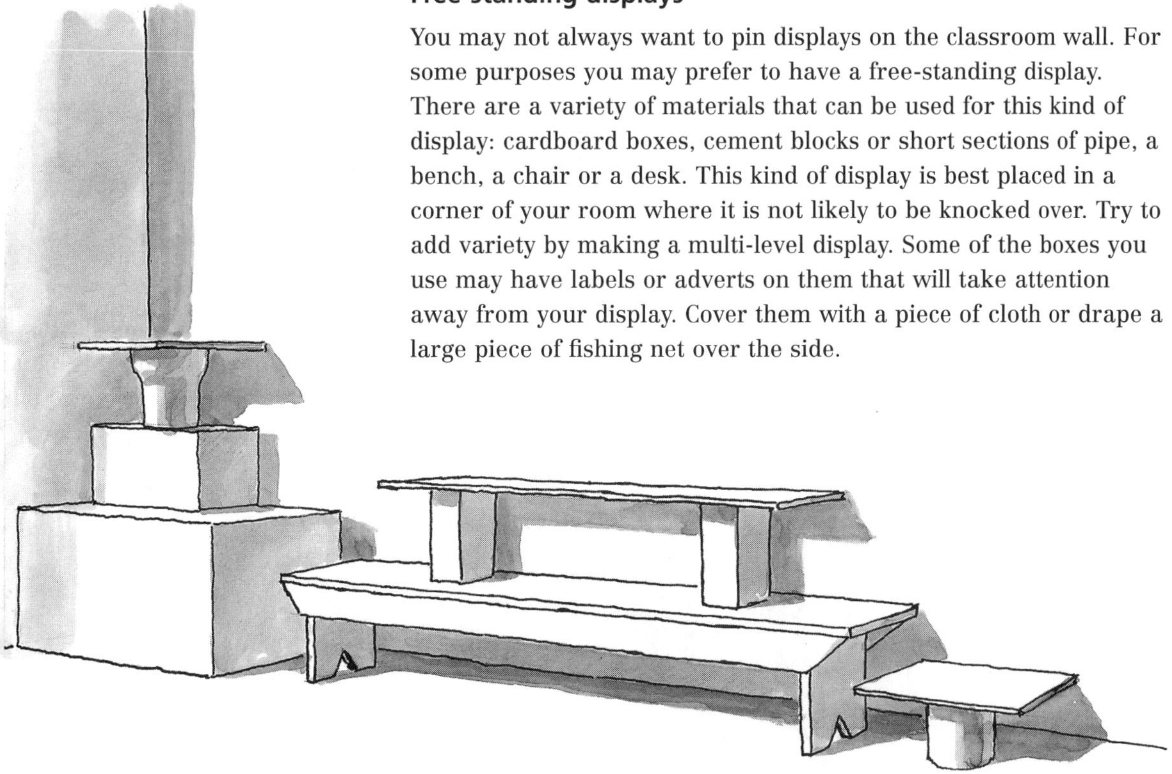

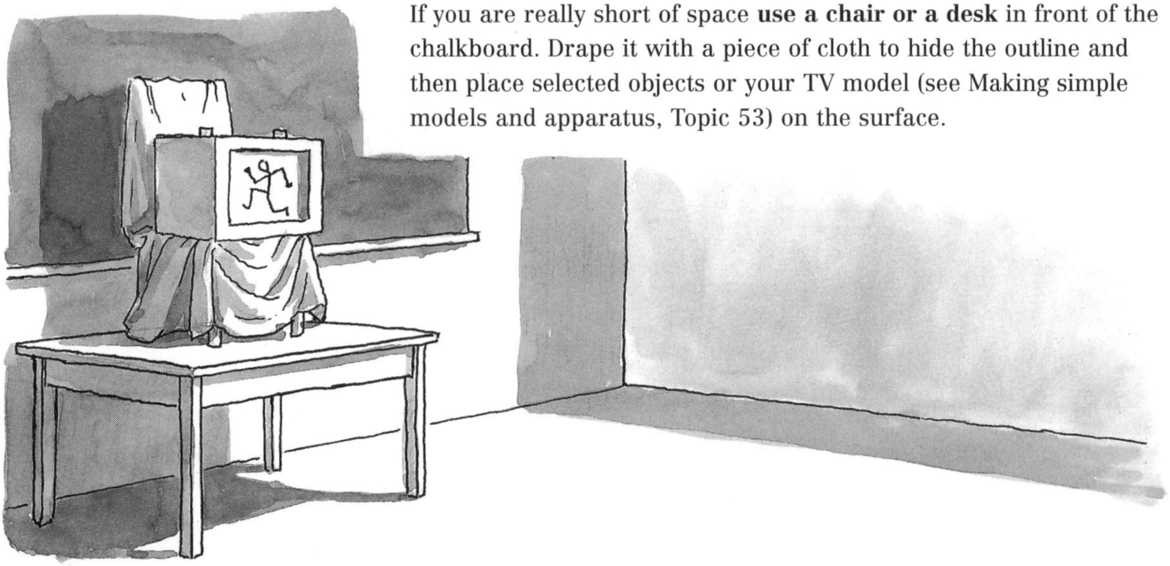

If you are really short of space **use a chair or a desk** in front of the chalkboard. Drape it with a piece of cloth to hide the outline and then place selected objects or your TV model (see Making simple models and apparatus, Topic 53) on the surface.

Can you use the ceiling?

Your ceiling may have exposed beams. These can be used to display work from rope or wire. If not, try to run a strong piece of string across the room.

What about the verandahs, windows or the area outside your room?

Corridors and verandahs are not ideal because of the number of people that move along them. Dust, dirt and even rain gets blown in. It may however be possible to use the area immediately around your door to make a small display to welcome parents on Open Day or to mark a religious holiday.

If you have glass windows you can make a display of silhouettes, to show art work or Maths shapes. They are particularly effective as a background for patterns and shapes made from coloured plastic paper. If these are stuck onto the window with Sellotape the light will shine through like a stained glass window.

You may also be able to use the area immmediately outside your classroom. You might choose to display some of the work your pupils have done. (See Using the school compound, Topic 57.) You could also try to make a small garden. Try making a theme garden, e.g. plants that grow on sand or in water. Make your own experimental plots. There may be a local botanical garden that can help or a keen gardener amongst your parents.

Labels

Be imaginative about the labels for your display, (lettering is discussed in Topic 52, Teaching aids). You could also make labels to match the theme of the display, e.g. from feathers, small thin sticks, or cut out letters from a newspaper.

The problem of shared classrooms

In schools working a double shift, teachers have to share their classroom with another group. This should **not** prevent teachers from displaying pupils' work. Where another teacher shares the afternoon shift, **plan ahead**. Persuade that teacher to work on the same theme with you. There is no reason why both classes should not contribute to the display. This may be one solution to problems of security. If classes from both the morning and afternoon sessions are involved in the work, pupils will have an interest in looking after the display and making sure that nothing disappears.

Security

In many schools there are security problems after school closes. This is a more difficult problem to solve. There is probably one room in the school that can be locked at night. The answer may be to make portable displays that fold up or can be easily packed away in a box (see Teaching aids, Topic 52). The display can then be placed in that room at the end of each day. There is, however, a limit to how much can be locked away. Encourage pupils and their parents to be proud of their classroom and their school. Give parents opportunities to come and see your work regularly (not just on an Open Day). It is important that everyone understands that the quality of your teaching and the learning of your pupils suffer when teaching aids and display materials are stolen.

56 Making the best use of limited resources

> ***Activity** What is in the local paper apart from local news?*
>
> Group your pupils and ask them to find out what is in each of the following categories and describe how the material is presented.
>
> Advertisements
>
> Weather
>
> Letters, cartoons and games
>
> Photographs
>
> Stories
>
> Currency information
>
> International news, radio and television programmes

In Topic 49, Assessing your resources, a chart was made of resources that may be available in your area. These included recycled materials as well as items that could be used to give more variety to activities in your lessons. This topic looks at the way that one commonly available resource material – your local newspaper – can be used to develop a variety of lessons across the curriculum.

Newspapers

Here are some suggestions for classwork activities in Social Studies and English.

You will need two copies of two different local newspapers published on the same day (which will not necessarily be the day you use them), for each of your groups. (Ask local banks, offices, your local Education Office or parents if they would let you have copies of their newspapers at the end of the week.)

Class discussion

- Why do we have newspapers?
- Who are the people who work on newspapers?
- What is a journalist?
- How can you become a journalist? If there is someone in your area who writes for a newspaper ask that person to come to the school and talk about his/her job to the class.
- What is the difference between writing for a newspaper and writing a story? (Compare a newspaper item with a unit in either the English or Environment Studies textbook.)

> ***Homework activity** Making up headlines*
>
> Ask pupils to listen to the news on the radio or TV and make their own headlines for the news that day.

Finding out about newspapers

What is a headline?

- Identify the headlines.
- How do headlines differ from ordinary sentences? Groups should cut different headlines from the paper and display them. In what way are they different?

> ***Activity** Vocabulary*
>
> - Find the meaning of: editor, column, headline, reporter, print, advertisement, deadline.
> - Let your pupils fill in the crossword in the children's section. Can they make a crossword from the words listed above?

Are newspaper reports accurate or biased?

- Try to find the same item in two different papers and ask pupils to compare the way that they are reported. (Reports on political news or an accident are usually best for this activity.)
- Which account was more accurate? Do they think that the reporter agreed with one side of the story rather than the other? Compare the newspaper to the same item on radio or TV.

Activity Writing for a newspaper

Let pupils begin to write articles that could be included in a class/school newspaper.

- Write a report of a school event.
- Write a story about a fire, a robbery or a local football match.
- Write an interview with the head or one of the teachers.

Activity How could you use a newspaper to develop each of the following Maths topics?

Calculating perimeter or area

Counting and estimating

Drawing graphs

Calculating averages

Activity Publish your own class or school newspaper

- Form groups – each group to be responsible for a different section.
- Discuss the work each group will do, e.g. research, writing articles, designing the layout, writing advertisement.
- Who will read the paper?
- How will you display it?

Using newspapers for curriculum activities

- Work on the vocabulary would make a good project in English.
- There are a number of Maths exercises that can be developed.
- Which group can get the most children standing on one sheet of newspaper? (Problem solving)

- Printing: Use local traditional symbols to stamp a design on cloth or paper. Cut the shape on a thick piece of yam or wood and dip it into some paint or a thick dye made from local materials. Use letter stamps to print a message or make a poster. (Art and Craft)
- Papier mâché made from old newspaper and flour and water paste can be used to make beads or small bowls for Maths and Science lessons.
- Collect articles on pollution and the environment. (Science)
- Look for advertisments for new technology, e.g. radios, fuel-efficient stoves. (Technology)

57 Using the school compound

Activity The school compound

In Topic 49, Assessing your resources you are asked to make a list of all the resources available to you. The resources in and around your school compound can be of immense value. Take time to assess what they are and how you can use them.

- What kind of trees/shrubs are there? Do you know their names? (Science/Environment Studies)
- How many different shapes (triangles/rectangles/angles, etc.) can you find on buildings/or fencing? (Maths)
- Look at the surface. Can you find different types of soil? Is there evidence of erosion? (Environment Studies, Science)

Make a list of all the features you might use and topics in the syllabus that they can be linked to.

Some schools with insufficient classrooms use the school compound as extra classroom space. Others use the area only during the break time or for Physical Education and Games lessons. Apart from these activities the area is often ignored. With a little imagination you can use resources in your compound to enrich topics in almost every subject in the curriculum. Learn to make the most of this valuable resource.

English and language ideas

Play **The alphabet game** in English or a local language using only objects seen in the playground area.

Discussion/imaginative writing

What I would do to improve the playground area or my school. Link this to Health and Life Skills.

Science and Environment studies

A nature trail

Take pupils on an observation walk around the compound at different times of the year. Make a list of things you would like pupils to look for and some questions for them to answer – **Where can you find....? What do you notice about....?** Use this activity for studying plants or insects, learning about angles and shapes or a weather study.

A soil survey

Collect a bucket of soil from the playground. Tip the contents on to a large piece of plastic or some newspaper. Collect any insects in a jar. Count the stones and arrange them in order of size. Put plants, (grass, seeds, flowers or twigs) in a separate pile. Use this information to make graphs or maps. This can be linked to Maths – shapes and spaces, counting (seeds, stones etc.) – and Geography.

A simple soil analysis

Put some soil in a jar with a lid, add water and shake the jar vigorously. Groups can observe what happens after 30 minutes, after

Ants – friend or enemy?

- How many different types of ant are there in the school compound?
- What local names do they have? (sugar ants, soldier ants, termites)?
- Study different types of ants' nests. Are ants useful or a nuisance?
- What do ants eat? Carry out an experiment: leave different scraps of food on a large leaf (cooked rice, some sugar, bread). How long does it take the ants to find the food? What do they do with the food?

Activity *Design a worksheet for water activities*

- How long does it take for puddles to disappear? (Link this with a lesson or discussion on evaporation.) Use the puddle to study ripples and reflections.
- Study the way flood water can carry soil and stones. Measure the width and depth of gullies that may have developed near classroom buildings. Collect samples of the size of stones and the type of soil at different points along the gully. (These can be linked with a discussion on storm damage and erosion.)

two hours, at the end of the school day and at the end of the second day. Ask pupils to make drawings of the different layers of soil that they see as the material gradually settles in the jar. Different groups can analyse soil from different parts of the playground, e.g. from an area used to grow flowers or vegetables, or from an area that is flooded after a storm.

- An experimental garden can be used for growing food crops in small beds under different conditions (Science).
- Study small animals, e.g. ants, spiders cockroaches or weevils.

You can make a similar study of mosquitoes, lizards and butterflies, or birds like the crow or weaver bird.

Water

(See also Project work, Topic 48.)

In most school compounds there will be some areas gradually becoming worn into a gully during heavy rain and other areas that become waterlogged and covered by large puddles after a storm. (Suggested activities are in the Activity box, left.)

A study of local weather (clouds, wind and rain)

- Make a sketch of the clouds seen each day for a week, in the morning, at noon and in the evening (or for a week at the beginning of the rainy season and again at the end of the rainy season).
- Find the names of the different cloud formations. Which ones are most common during the dry season? Which are most common during the rainy season?
- Link your study with the weather forecast in your local newspaper. Is the forecast in the paper usually accurate for your area? Can your pupils begin to make a weather forecast from their own observations? (Use Topic 53, Making simple models and apparatus to help you make observations.)

Health and life skills

- Use the compound to teach pupils about health and safety.
- Ask them to draw a map of their compound. (Older classes can make a drawing to scale.)
- Discuss how different areas can be used for a variety of activities, e.g. Games and Dance.
- Plot areas of potential danger, e.g. stagnant pools of water that provide a breeding ground for mosquitoes; food and rubbish thrown around the compound or left in the classroom (linked to cockroaches or rats).
- Encourage pupils to find ways of making the school compound more attractive. Work with other teachers to begin a project that will also involve parents.

58 Using the local area

Cultural studies

- Local history, traditions and festivals.
- Studies of people – where they have come from, their language or their jobs.
- Maps and plans.
- Local work and industry.

Language lessons

- Reading – street signs, road symbols or advertisements.
- Interviews.
- A collection of stories or poems.

Science

- Daily observations of weather; wind direction, cloud formation and rainfall.
- Seasonal changes in the natural vegetation or the farming calendar.
- Studies of plants, animals, birds and insects.

Maths

- Traffic studies (graphs) data handling of all kinds of information, e.g. types of illnesses, market prices, etc.

Technology

- Local technology; brick-making, pottery, weaving or metal work.

Linking the local area to the curriculum

Whether your school is situated in a rural area, a village or a town the local environment is a rich resource that can be used for a variety of lessons including Science, Technology, Environment/Social Studies, or History. Using knowledge from the local area helps pupils develop a greater understanding not only of their own community but also of their region, their country and the world they live in. Lessons using the local area as a source of information can be linked to topics in the syllabus and should encourage pupils to observe and investigate, to ask questions and to develop opinions.

The project below could be carried out in the local area around the school (see Project work, Topic 48 and Working with the community, Topic 69).

Local buildings

A study of local buildings may be used in a project linked to topics in both the English and Environment studies syllabus. As you come to school each day you may see other buildings of particular interest that can be studied.

- Group activities should based on pupils observing, measuring, drawing and finding out. Each group should be given one activity from the chart below and should be asked to write a summary of their findings, to make drawings and where possible collect samples of materials.

Suggested group activities based on the survey of local buildings

Group 1	Group 2	Group 3
Make labelled drawings of their observations. • What are the buildings made of? Cement blocks, brick, wood, or other local materials. • Roofing materials: tiles, galvanised sheets. • Windows: glass/ shutters. • Security: walls/ iron bars	What are the buildings used for? • Homes. • Shops. • Services, e.g. banks or petrol stations. • Local industries. • More than one purpose. Have any changes been made to the buildings?	Learn about the history of the town. • How long has it been in existence? • Why do people live there? • Famous people from the town. • Important local festivals.

Suggested group activities based on the survey of local buildings		
Group 4 Facilities: • Type of road, gutters/drainage. • Amount of rubbish nearby – how is it removed? • Water electricity and telephones. • Transport.	**Group 5** Find out about the people who live/work in the area. • Where do they come from? • What language/s do they speak? • What jobs do they do?	**Group 6** Find out about services in the area. • Shops? • Police Station? • Hospital or clinics? • Schools? • Markets? • Lorry/train stations?

Make a display of the information at the end of the study (Displaying pupils' work, Topic 55.) with a map of the area made by the pupils. Their information can be displayed around the map, illustrated with drawings or samples of materials. A well-presented display stimulates interest and should lead to other areas of investigation.

More challenging activities

After completing all the fact-finding activities, pupils in more senior classes should be able to list the main problems affecting people living and working in the area, e.g. poor drainage, lack of transport. You might also develop more detailed studies of local history; link studies to Technology topics by learning about local building techniques; or to environmental issues such as disposing of waste or the local water supply.

Encourage pupils to make suggestions for changes that would improve their local environment. (See also Project work, Topic 48 and Stretching able children, Topic 36.) You may be able to carry out some of their suggestions with the help of parents, elders or the local authority.

Your local area may include important geographical features. Work with other teachers to develop resource material about these features, e.g. your school may be situated near:

- an important river (link this with a study of erosion, farming and fishing activities or trade routes).
- a range of hills or near a mountain (differences in climate and vegetation, water supply, soil erosion, or the distribution of population).
- a forest area (carry out a small tree count, look at the commercial or medicinal value of individual trees, study the animal life or local farming).

59 The purpose of assessment

Assessment serves a very valuable purpose. It can be used to identify the individual learning needs of pupils (see Teaching strategies, Section 5), and to help you improve your own teaching skills (Reflection, Topic 7).

Assessment skills

In order to make a fair assesment you must be able to:

- Assess whether pupils have unerstood your lessons. This can be done through observation, questions during the lesson, and evidence from classwork, exercises and tests.
- Recognise the individual levels of ability and achievement that each pupil is able to reach.
- Set targets to improve learning achievement.

How should assessment be carried out?

- **Collect** information.
- **Evaluate** that information.
- Use the information to make **your teaching and the learning of your pupils more effective**.

Collecting information

Always try to collect evidence of achievement and progress in a way that is useful not only for yourself but also for your colleagues, the school, your pupils and their parents. Most teachers keep records of the marks their pupils have gained when class work, homework or tests have been completed, (Topic 65, Keeping records). Other methods of evaluation and assessment can also provide useful information, e.g. when teachers are asked to complete continuous assessment sheets at the end of the year. This section will suggest ways in which you might make more use of observation to collect information on your pupils.

Observation

There is probably very little time during the day when you are not observing one or more of your pupils either formally or informally. It is useful to learn how to record this information properly but you will need to organise time for this activity.

Definition of assessment

- Assessment is a process of evaluation.

There are a variety of ways in which schools can measure the progress and achievement of their pupils.

- Test and examinations.

These assess specific pieces of work daily, weekly, termly or at the end of each year.

- Cumulative records or continuous assessment.

These record all aspects of learning and include records of family details, health, class work, attitudes and behaviour as well as test results.

Activity *Time for observation*

Note the times when you might find time to observe pupils informally.

During lessons.

In the playground during breaktimes.

During practical work.

During extra-curricular activities, e.g. during games or club activities.

Other times.

Using web diagrams for assessment

These can be used to chart pupil attitudes and skill. Prepare a sheet for each pupil and add to it gradually, picking out pupils' good and bad points.

Be aware of exactly what you are looking for

You need to observe attitudes and behaviour as well as knowledge and skills. A number of areas are listed below. You may have others you want to add.

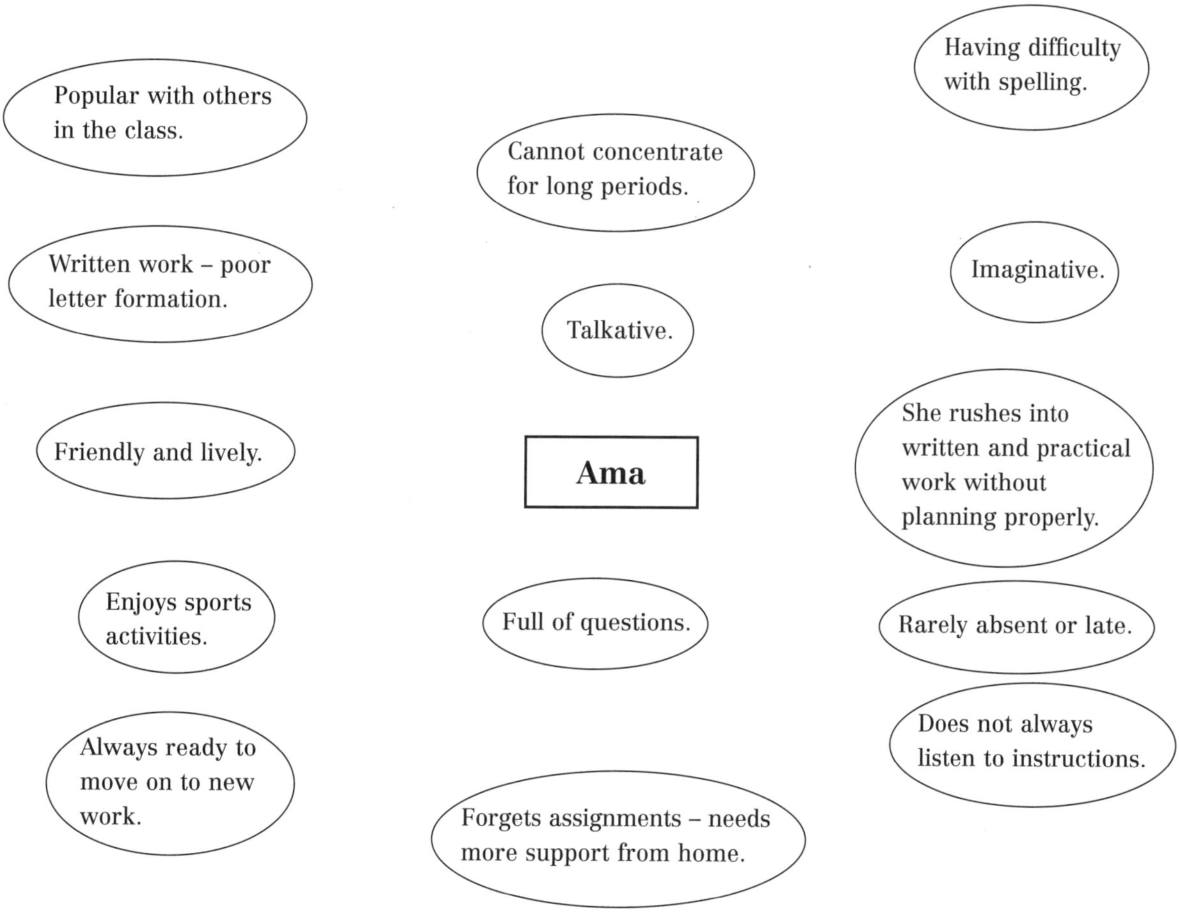

1 The diagram can show: Attitudes and behaviour

- Behaviour with other pupils – boys and girls.
- Attitude towards school and learning.
- Interaction with other people.

2 Knowledge and skills

- Remembering and understanding subject matter.
- Ability to solve problems.
- Practical work.

Activity Interpreting observations

Different interpretations might be made of the web being built on Ama. Each will require a slightly different solution.

Ama is a good student – but easily bored and distracted by things going on in the class.

Ama has good social skills but has limited academic ability.

Ama is rather immature for her age.

What would be your solution to each of these interpretations?

Evaluating the information

As information is added to each section of the web, you can begin to link comments together. This will allow you to give helpful advice to Ama and her parents in your term reports or during Open Day. Look at three comments that may have been noted at different times during the term:

Cannot concentrate for long periods.
Does not always listen to instructions.
She rushes into written and practical work without planning properly.

What do they tell you about Ama? How could you help her?

A more formal schedule for lesson observation may help answer some of these questions.

Name: **Ama** Boy/**Girl** Class .... Subject: **English (Record of lesson observations)**	
Time on Task	**Comments**
Preparing to work on set task.	Is never fully prepared for the lesson – forgets books or loses pencil.
Working on set tasks: Written work.	Has not learned to form letters clearly. Poor spelling – particularly with words containing more than two syllables.
Contributing to discussion.	Has interesting ideas and is always ready take part in discussion.
Talking with her group about the lesson or lesson activities.	Is often chosen to join groups but wastes a lot of time talking.
Practical work/Activities.	Untidy and disorganised.
Time off-task	**Comments**
Talking to other pupils.	Talks constantly.
Moving about the room.	Spends a lot of time looking at the work of others or coming to the teacher's desk.
Misbehaving.	Playful – takes other pupils' pencils/rubbers without asking.

Providing help

End of term reports and continuous assessment sheets are often completed hurriedly and the same type of comment is used:

Satisfactory but could do better.
A good reader.
Poor work should try harder.

These comments do not always provide the kind of information that can be used to improve achievement. 'How might the pupil '*do better*'? 'In what way is the work *poor*?' Perhaps the pupil is '*trying*' – but without much success.

Look at the suggestions made in the more detailed record of Ama's problems in English. Immediate practical help can be given to improve her writing skills. Here are some suggestions.

Name: Ama	**Subject: English**
Areas to improve	**Help**
1 Poor spelling – particularly with words containing 'ou' 'ie' and 'ai'. Confuses these with 'ow' 'ee' and 'a'.	1 Help her to make clear rules to improve her spelling. Find word games that will use letter combinations she is not clear about.
2 Has not learned to form letters clearly.	2 Observe the way she holds letters her pencil. Encourage her to draw picture patterns such as wavy lines or circles to improve pencil control and to trace letter shapes.

Other members of staff will have similar difficulties. Find time to share problems and ideas and try to build up a series of activities that will help your pupils.

60 Assessing pupils' progress and achievement

Definition

Structured observation: Making time for observation throughout the day, keeping notes of what you see.

(See The purpose of assessment, Topic 59. Activity: Time for observation)

In order to make a **continuous assessment** of pupil progress and achievement you will be expected to assess not only the knowledge and skills of your pupils, but also their attitudes and behaviour.

Assessing knowledge and skills

One of the first steps in this assessment is to find out how far each pupil has actually gained knowledge in a variety of subjects across the curriculum. Your Ministry may have outlined certain targets that pupils are expected to achieve in each subject. For example, in the Science syllabus, students are expected to understand that plants need light and water in order to grow properly.

What can your pupils do?

- Can they remember and understand what they have been taught?
- Can they use information to complete activities and practical work?
- Can they solve problems?

The quickest and most common method of assessing how much pupils remember is to ask **closed questions** that can be answered by a single word or a short sentence. You may also test understanding by asking **open-ended questions** requiring a more detailed answer, or by giving written work. Topic 61, Preparation for school tests and examinations gives further examples of the way that you can test the level of knowledge.

You will also find that **structured observation** is a useful method for assessing whether your pupils understand concepts or are able to use knowledge to complete assignments, carry out practical activities or to solve problems. (See The purpose of assessment, Topic 59.)

Assessing attitudes and behaviour

Your Ministry of Education will have outlined the kind of attitudes and behaviour expected from pupils, e.g. pupils should be helped to develop 'a life-long interest in learning' or a 'concern for the environment'.

Comments in continuous assessment reports are often related to attitudes or behaviour. These are frequently based on personal judgements made by teachers. In order to give a true reflection of each pupil's progress, it is important for you to develop a more systematic way of assessing and recording achievement in these areas.

Activity *What should you assess?*

- Behaviour with other pupils (during lessons, extra-curricular activities such as games or club activities or in the playground).
- Attitude to school.
- Attitude to new work.
- Participation in lesson activities (asking questions; joining discussions; practical work).
- Working individually; in groups; with the whole class.
- Attitudes towards taking responsibility.

The following example of a checklist will help you observe each pupil as an individual and will also help you to assess the way groups work together.

Group A **Number in Group 6**

Name of pupil *Ama*

Subject: Mathematics Measuring and Ordering

Task: To draw their foot prints, measure them and arrange them in order of size.

Criteria	
Makes a plan to do the activity.	✗
Willing to share materials.	✓
Talks.	✓
Listens.	✗
Waits for others to say what should be done.	✗
Relates to the group.	✓
Concentrates on the task.	✗
Makes sure the task is completed (not necessarily correctly).	✗
Loses interest once own foot has been drawn.	✓
Tidies up at the end of the activity.	✓

You might also assess individual attitudes and behaviour by keeping a checklist of attitudes that you or your school want to encourage.

Attitudes/behaviour	*Ama*
Tolerance	✓
Care for others	✓
Taking and accepting responsibility	✗
Working hard	✗
Neatness	✗
Politeness	✓
Punctuality	✓

61 Preparation for school tests and examinations

Activity *Designing a simple examination paper*

Design a simple examination paper to test the understanding of your students in the work covered in, e.g. Maths during a term. Use each of the following types of question.

- **The calculation of simple sums that show pupils understand mathematical processes:** Addition/subtraction, using whole numbers or fractions/calculation of area.
- **Sequencing:** Arrange in order of size, largest (or smallest) first. Add the next three numbers in this number line.
- **Problem-solving:** Add the largest to the smallest. Solve these story sums or find the missing number/s.

Example, The answer is 12. Make up one multiplication and one division sum for which this answer is true, e.g. (2 × 6, or 36 ÷ 3)

- **Angles and shapes:** A question that requires pupils to recognise or measure angles or geometrical shapes.

As part of the formal assessment process, almost all schools give regular tests and examinations. Teachers often give short weekly tests, to assess mastery of particular areas of knowledge. There are usually more formal end of term or end of year tests or examinations in core subjects. This section will review preparation for internal tests in primary schools. There are three tasks you need to complete.

- Preparing the test questions.
- Working out the marking schemes.
- Preparing pupils.

Make sure that the test is fair: that questions are not too easy and not too hard. (The majority of pupils should be able to pass.) It is best to work out questions with other teachers in the same year group. (See Working with other staff, Topic 66.) This makes the task easier and ensures that results are more consistent.

- Decide what topics are to be tested.
- How many questions will be asked?
- How long will the test/exam take?

Always give notice of tests: We will do 10 mental arithmetic questions on Monday, Wednesday and Friday. Our spelling tests will be on Tuesday and Thursday. Give pupils a timetable for end of term tests well in advance.

Preparing the questions

Writing good test questions takes practice. It is not always as easy as it seems. You will need to ask the questions in a variety of ways. Daily or weekly mental arithmetic and spelling tests usually ask short, direct questions, e.g. 'Spell **classroom**.' End of year examinations, especially for upper primary classes, will need questions that test both knowledge and understanding.

Avoid asking too many questions that need one-word answers. Your exam paper should provide a balance between **objective** questions, requiring a simple recall of facts and **subjective** questions that test the understanding of your pupils. Instead of asking a simple objective question: 'Name two ways that we can keep our environment clean', you might ask pupils 'Name two ways that we can keep our environment clean and give one reason why each activity is important.'

Every pupil should be able to gain two marks by answering the first part (using litter bins and cleaning the gutters). The second part allows pupils to think for themselves. They might say, 'Mosquitoes and flies breed in rubbish that is not covered and they carry diseases.' or 'If we do not clean the gutter there will be floods in the rainy season.'

Even short objective questions should make pupils think. Your pupils are more likely to do well in tests if you give them the chance to answer similar questions in your lessons.

Multi-choice questions

These are very commonly used to test pupils' knowledge and understanding.

The questions give a choice of three or four short answers, only one of which is right. Instead of writing the answer out, the pupil ticks the correct box, as in this example.

A thermometer is used to measure:
a) distance ☐
b) weight ☐
c) temperature ☐
d) length ☐

The pupils should put a tick in the **temperature** box. Tell your pupils that it is better to guess the answer than to leave boxes empty.

Preparing pupils for tests

Before the test or exam begins always give very clear instructions, verbally and on the exam paper (or on the board). You may still find that some pupils do not understand what they have to do. Ask if everyone understands and explain again if necessary.

Marking tests

- Work out a clear marking scheme and explain to your pupils how the marks will be given. This is another area where it is useful to work with teachers in the same year group. (See Working with other staff, Topic 66.) When you set the questions, give marks that are multiples of 10 (they are easier to make into a percentage when you fill in your records). Give pupils clear pointers about the best way for them to gain marks. Remember that your main purpose is to find out what they know.
- Make brief comments on the paper to indicate where pupils have lost marks.
- Keep clear records of marks. Design a grid that will be easy to fill in and will allow you to see at a glance the progress of each pupil. (See Keeping records, Topic 65.)

62 Preparing pupils for external examinations

***Activity** Planning revision*

- Go through the syllabus of each subject to be examined and make a list of important topics that you will need to revise with your pupils.
- Look at past examination papers and make a note of the different ways that questions may be asked.
- Ask pupils to make their own list of topics they feel they know and topics needing more revision.

In some areas pupils are required to sit an external examination at the end of primary or junior secondary school in order to get a place in a senior secondary school. The Ministry of Education or an Examinations Council normally sets the papers and most teachers try to prepare their students by letting them practise past papers. Unfortunately, this method does not always result in a high level of passes. The best way to help your students is to show them how to revise. (These methods will help pupils taking school tests and examinations as well.)

- How to make revision notes.
- How to answer different types of question and to fill in answer sheets.
- The way marks can be gained.
- The importance of timing.
- The need for checking through answers.

Prepare a timetable

Your pupils will need to plan their revision time. Revision should start at least one month before the examination. Help your students make a timetable that will cover revision of all the major topics before the examination day.

Teach pupils how to make revision notes

Model answers/compositions are not really helpful. They often prevent students from putting down their own ideas. Encourage your pupils to make **brief** notes of the important points needed to answer each question. The more past questions they try, the more confident your students will feel.

Make use of peer support

In the activity students were asked to make a list of topics they feel that they know and topics needing more revision. Go through their lists carefully and pair a good student with a weaker one. (A friend can sometimes explain a difficult topic more easily than the teacher.)

Gaining marks in written questions

Explain to your pupils that marks are given not only for the correct answer but also for the thinking process. They should show how they worked out the answer. This is particularly important in Mathematics exams but is equally useful when writing compositions.

Filling in answer sheets

Some exams are based on multiple choice questions and an answer sheet is provided. These can be very difficult to understand the first time they are used. Try and get a copy of an official answer sheet to show your pupils. If this is not available draw a sample copy on the board and show pupils how to fill it in.

Sample answer sheet

Name:				Exam No.				School			
Q1	A	B	C	Q5	A	B	C	Q9	A	B	C
Q2	A	B	C	Q6	A	B	C	Q10	A	B	C
Q3	A	B	C	Q7	A	B	C	Q11	A	B	C
Q4	A	B	C	Q8	A	B	C	Q12	A	B	C

During the examination

- **Stress the importance of timing**. It is very easy for pupils to get stuck answering one question and then to find that there is not enough time left to answer the rest of the questions properly. In multiple choice tests (such as those given as an entrance examination for secondary school) the score is based on the number of questions answered correctly.
- Tell the students to: **answer all the questions** as quickly as possible. Mark the answers on to the answer sheet straight away.
- **Make a guess** at the more difficult questions. **Circle these questions on the question paper.**
- **Go back** if they have time. Try the more difficult questions again.
- **Make sure all questions have been answered**.
- **Leave five minutes to check through**. Marks can easily be lost if part of a question has been left out, if the answer sheet has not been filled in correctly, if the student numbers a question wrongly or even fails to put his or her name or number on the paper.

Counselling

Think about your students and how they feel about the exam they are going to take. It is an important point in their school life and they will naturally feel nervous. Remind them of all the revision they have done and tell them that you are confident that they will do well. Don't forget to wish them 'Good Luck' before they go to the examination.

63 Making marking more effective

Most teachers complain that they have too much marking and with classes of 40 or more pupils, marking a composition or 10 sums for each pupil will take a lot of time.

What is the purpose of marking?

Many of your reasons will apply equally to the purpose of assessment (see Topic 59). Marking is used to check pupils' knowledge and understanding.

- Have pupils understood new ideas (concepts) presented in the content of the lesson?
- Do they know the correct method to use to solve a problem?
- Are they using their chosen method correctly?
- Can they use their knowledge to solve similar problems?

Marking class work and homework exercises gives you vital clues to the particular difficulties that each of your pupils is experiencing. It will also give you feedback on your teaching.

Activity *Marking a project*

Why do teachers mark work? List as many reasons as you can.

If you are marking projects or practical work you will need a clear marking scheme that gives credit for different types of effort. You will need to give marks for:

Content: has the pupil provided the information needed to complete the project or exercise properly?

Accuracy: has the pupil got the correct result?

Art work: some pupils are much more skilled than others, they deserve credit but others should not be penalised because they cannot draw well.

Research: is there any evidence that the pupil has tried to find extra information?

What do you need to find out?

Mathematics and English textbooks usually provide a series of exercises to test whether pupils have understood the lesson. As a teacher you undoubtedly spend many hours marking these exercises but does this really give you the information that you need in order to help correct mistakes?

It is possible to find out much more about the problems your pupils are facing by marking a few examples more effectively.

- What are the particular **kinds of mistake** being made? (See Helping individual pupils, Topic 35.)
- **Which pupils** make these mistakes? (See Helping individual pupils, Topic 35.)
- Does each pupil **understand** the mistake he/she is making? (Assessing pupils' progress and achievement, Topic 60.)

How many examples **do you need to mark** in order to get an awareness of individual problems? Look at the Activity which shows sums taken from a completed subtraction exercise.

Allow pupils to mark their own work

Topic 4, The process of learning stresses that pupils should become more responsible for their own progress and achievement. Even though you have overall responsibility for marking and assessing

Activity *Find the problem*

42	51	65	90	44	76
−25	−37	−19	−42	−26	−58
27	24	46	52	18	22

Can you explain **why** some sums are wrong? What mistakes are being made in the subtraction process?

Although these are all subtraction sums, in example 1: the pupil has added the 5 and the 2 in the units column (perhaps because the 5 is larger than the 2 – does he/she understand about 'borrowing'?); and in example 4 the pupil seems to be unsure what to do if there is a '0' in the sum.

Can **pupils** explain **the steps** that they used and where they went wrong?

pupils' work, you can still involve them in the task of working out marking schemes and with marking some exercises.

- This will make them more critical of their own work.
- It will help to reinforce their learning.

Will they cheat?

There is no point in cheating if pupils know that you do not intend to record marks gained in **every exercise**.

'They won't do all the exercises'

What does 10/40 or 34/40 really tell you? You want to know why the pupil is getting something wrong not **how many times** he/she gets it wrong.

Setting up a useful marking scheme

Most pupils like to see the grade or mark that they have received. It is probably the first thing that they look at. Some do not look any further than that. Teachers ask them to do their corrections but it may not be entirely clear what needs correcting. They may simply copy the correct work from someone else. Make comments in the side margin or at the bottom of the exercise that pinpoint the exact nature of the errors that have occurred. Make sure that what you write is helpful and not critical.

64 Coping with marking in large classes

> ***Activity** Working out what you have to do*
>
> How many exercises do you give each week that require marking by you?
>
> How many hours do you spend marking each week? Do you feel this is too much or too little?
>
> How many exercises do you set that have one word to mark?
>
> How often do you set a composition or a written exercise?
>
> What sort of work do you mark?
>
> - Spelling
> - Composition
> - Maths
> - Other
>
> When and where do you do your marking?
>
> - In class
> - During free periods or the lunch-break at school
> - Before or after school starts
> - At home

This is a particularly difficult task for teachers. There is only a certain amount that you can realistically be expected to do.

You have probably found, particularly if you have a large class, that many of your class exercises only ask questions requiring one word answers. You will have found that these are useful to make a quick assessment of the learning. However, if you want your pupils to gain a better understanding of their lessons, you will have to set some exercises that require more detailed answers. Without practice at writing longer answers your pupils will not be able to develop their writing skills or their reasoning.

How can you mark more effectively?

Pupils can be given more responsibility for correcting work. Look at Topic 63, Making marking more effective. Can you adapt or extend some of those ideas to make your marking less of burden for you and more meaningful for your pupils? Pupils can certainly help to mark some of the short one-word answer exercises.

Marking Maths

Keep the number of examples short and ask pupils to exchange work with a partner, or around the group. Write a list of common errors on the board and ask partners to find out **where** particular mistakes have been made. This will help to improve their own understanding. (See Making marking more effective, Topic 63.)

Marking compositions

This is a task that many primary teachers dread. Marking 50 or 60 individual compositions is very time-consuming. Unless you are able to discuss faults individually, the chances are that pupils will only look at the mark they have been given and fail to think about ways of improving their writing. It is important for pupils to learn to write a composition that is both grammatically correct and interesting. This skill can be built up gradually by focusing on one element of composition writing at a time.

- **Find the most interesting story:** Begin by letting each group choose the best story in their group. This can be read aloud to the class, passed to other groups to read or be pinned on the wall. Ask each group to choose one story from their group and combine their efforts to make improvements. Again the class can judge the most interesting group story.

This kind of assessment will take a whole period to do effectively but can result in greater improvements in the writing of compositions than individual marking by the teacher.

- **Improve written work and spelling:** Pupils frequently misspell certain words. Before asking the class to write a composition, discuss the kind of words they might like to use and list them at the side of the board as a reference. Encourage pupils to use unusual words (verbal skills may well be more advanced than spelling skills). Ask them to write the initial letter or leave gaps for words they cannot spell.
- **Correct grammatical errors:** Use a code to show errors. Make a poster of your code and display it in the classroom. Add some of your own symbols to show other common mistakes that occur in your class.

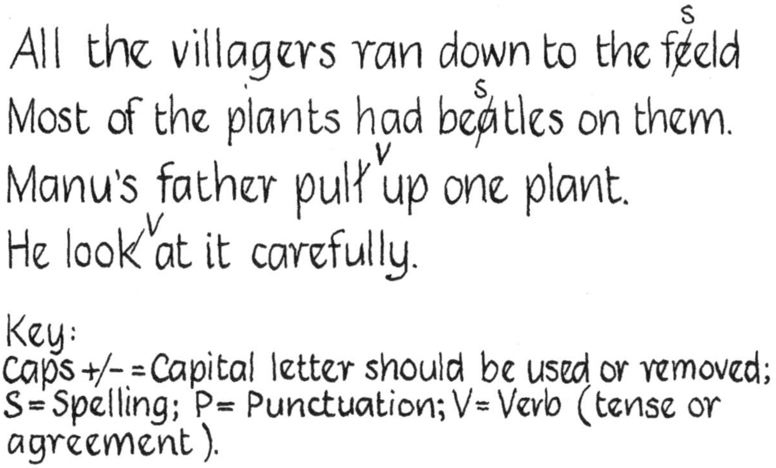

You might also use words like *Meaning* where the meaning is not clear; *Sentence* where the sentence does not make sense; *Detail* where further information is needed to complete the answer.

Combine writing compositions with work in other subjects

1. Environment Studies: Pupils might write a composition on the way they would like to improve their school/village.
2. Cultural Studies: pupils could write about an elderly person in the village (their character or their life) or find out the history of a local festival.

How to improve your speed

A great deal of your marking will be correcting whether something is right or wrong. Improve your speed and spend less time on this.

- Give short class exercises or tests of no more than 10 questions.
- Use simple questions that require a short sentence (to test recall).
- Pupils can help by writing answers to each question on a separate line. (Divide pages in their exercise book down the middle in order to save space.) They can also underline each answer.

65 Keeping records

> ***Activity** Personal records*
>
> Here is a list of some of the more personal records that have been developed by primary teachers. Which do you keep? Are there any others that you have found useful?
>
> - Information on each pupil's home background.
> - Details of their hobbies and interests.
> - Books that pupils have read.
> - Reading, spelling or Maths attainment levels.
> - Activities and tasks or project work completed.
> - Homework assignments given during each week.
> - Test and examination questions used in various subjects.
> - Observation of behaviour and attitudes.

Records are a very important part of the assessment process as they help to build up a clear picture of the progress and achievement of each pupil in your class. Without them you will be unable to help your pupils improve or to give their parents information that will encourage them to become involved in the learning of their children.

In many countries in Africa, Ministries of Education now ask schools to carry out a continuous assessment of pupils' work. This involves recording both formal tests and records of class work and homework. It also includes making an assessment of their behaviour and attitude to work. Teachers are usually provided with assessment sheets for the end of term reports but you may feel that you need to find different ways of keeping your own personal records so that you can gradually build up the information you need.

What records do class teachers need to keep?

Some are part of the regulations required by your Ministry of Education.

- Records of attendance.
- Stock lists.
- Schemes of work and lesson plans.
- Continuous assessment records.

How should records be kept?

The system you use should be **clear, simple** and **systematic**, one that can be easily understood by other members of staff, the pupils themselves and their parents. It is a good idea to work with other teachers in your year group. (See Working with other staff, Topic 66.) Decide what information you need to collect and agree on the way that you will all keep these records. (You will find examples of different types of records in other sections of this book.)

> ***Activity** Folders*
>
> Create a folder for each pupil in your class. You can glue or staple a sheet of manila paper into the shape of a folder.
>
> When each record sheet has been completed date it and put it in the folder.

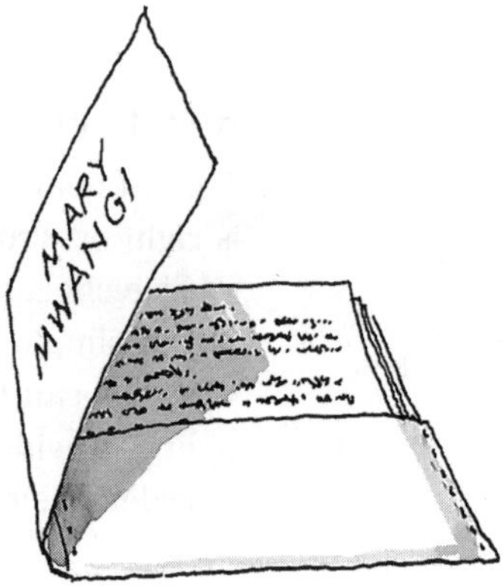

Records of examination marks

Whilst continuous assessment records build up a picture of each pupil it is not always easy to see the overall progress of the class. An examination 'Master Sheet' can provide this information.

The example illustrated shows the attainment of each child in each subject. It is useful for you, as the class teacher, for your head or an inspector and for the parents of your pupils.

Examination Master Sheet............ 2000							
Term............		**Class..............**		**Name of Teacher**			
Name	**English**	**Maths**	**Science**	**Local Language**	**Art/Craft**	**Environment Studies**	**Pupil average**
Adam	54%	52%	61%	65%	44%	36%	312/600 52.%
Kwesi	46%	42%	38%	50%	53%	47%	276/600 46.%
Abena	63%	44%					
Elizabeth	65%	68%					
Class Total	228	206					
Average	**57%**	**51.5%**					

Analysing the information

Subject columns show the performance of each pupil in each subject. You can use this, together with the Class average to:

1. get an indication of overall attainment of the class in that subject.
2. reflect on the examination itself. Were questions too easy/too hard?
3. identify your own strengths and weakness as a teacher. For instance you may notice that pupils always get good results in English and Environment Studies in your class, but seem to do less well in Maths.

Individual pupil performance can be followed along the rows. These also show the overall performance of each pupil in relation to other members of the class.

Section 9 Working with others

66 Working with other staff

Teachers are expected to work with other members of staff or as a member of a team. Many schools have Subject teams that meet regularly to decide on programmes for a particular subject but there are also opportunities for teachers to work with other colleagues teaching the same year group. It may even be possible to work with a colleague who teaches in your classroom during the morning or afternoon shift.

Advantages of working with a colleague

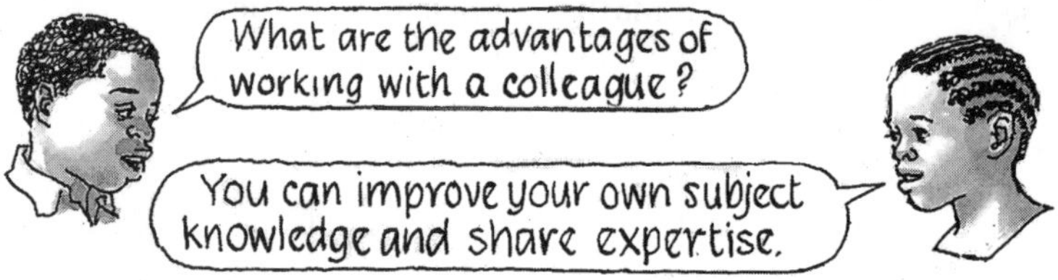

Interests and skills

You might start by making a list of the skills or interests of each member of your year group. That way you will know where to ask for help. The teacher in Class 2A, for example, might be a good artist and would be pleased to do the artwork for displays if another teacher would help him or her to prepare some lessons or worksheets. You can learn from each other.

> ***Activity** What do other teachers do?*
>
> - How do they encourage pupils who never contribute to lessons?
> - How do they make sure that group work activities provide for the needs of pupils with different levels of ability?
> - How do they teach reading and writing skills?

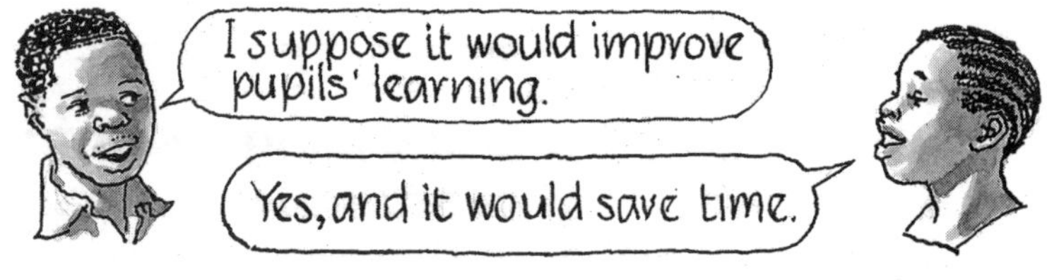

Management

Discuss issues of concern in the management of learning in your classes. This would ensure that all the classes in your year group covered the same amount of the syllabus.

> ***Activity** Discuss ways to improve*
>
> - Lesson plans.
> - Activities.
> - Problem-solving skills.
> - Questioning skills.
>
> Take notes as you discuss the various problems with other staff. Share your ideas.

Sharing the work load

Organise your time together. Even half an hour at the end of an afternoon each week will build up a considerable amount of information and material by the end of the term.

Most schools have more than one class in each year group. Some members of the group may be experienced teachers who have had an opportunity to teach the syllabus many times before. Others may be young teachers with less experience of the syllabus but perhaps with new ideas for teaching particular topics. Topic 17, Schemes of work and Topic 18, Lesson plans have some suggestions on collaboration.

Decide together who will prepare provisional lesson plans for topics covered during the first half of the term. This collaboration is very useful where teachers may have taken specialist courses in different subjects.

List suitable activities for each topic and let each teacher organise and collect the resources for one of these activities. Other teachers in the group can then use the material during their lesson.

Sharing resources

This will follow on from a shared preparation of resources for learning activities, for example making teaching aids such as flash cards and poster displays together. See Topics 49, Assessing your resources and 50, Collecting and storing resources for suggestions on useful items to collect and ways in which to store resources in the classroom. Storage space is usually very scarce and it makes more sense to share rather than to duplicate collections.

At the beginning of the year, have a meeting with year group colleagues and make a list of the resources that you have and decide who will keep the items. Keep a record sheet in each class. Classes from other year groups may want to borrow your resources so make sure that the record is filled in when each item is borrowed and returned. At the end of the year take time to look at all the items and replace or repair materials as necessary.

Record of Resources for Year 2

Resources	Location	Borrowed by/Date	Returned/Comment
Templates	Class 2B		
Containers for measuring liquids	Class 2A	Class 1/18th Sept.	20th September
Maps	Class 2B		
Cardboard boxes	Class 2B	Class 3/5th October display	In use for a project
Newspapers	Class 2A	Class 2B/9th October	To be replaced

67 Parents and teachers

***Activity** How does your school keep in contact with parents?*

- Does your school have a plan for making contact with the parents/guardians of pupils in your class either through formal or informal meetings?
- How many of the parents/guardians of pupils in your class have you met this year?
- How many parents/guardians have come more than once?
- Are there any that have never come at all?
- What do you do to encourage parents/guardians to come to your class?

Parents have a very clear role to play in the education of their children and in the work of the school. It is important to establish regular links between the home and the school.

Among the pupils in your class there will be some whose parents are keen to learn about the progress of their children. There will be others, however, who seem to have very little interest in what their child is doing and never visit the school. Some parents will be unable to read or write and may feel they cannot help their children with school work. Those parents in particular will need to be encouraged to take an interest in their child's progress in school.

Your first meeting with the parents/guardians of pupils in your class may be on an informal basis during an Open Day, or at a Parent-Teachers Meeting. (See also Topic 69, Working with the community.) During that time you should make an effort to talk with parents from your class and let them feel that you welcome their interest and support.

Meeting parents/guardians

Your attitude to parents/guardians can make a lot of difference to their interest in the school.

Parents need to understand that you welcome their visits and expect to see them regularly. You might suggest that they try to visit your class at the end of each term. If they are very busy or live some distance from the school you will need to arrange to see them at a time that is suitable for both of you. As many classes are very large each interview should last not more than 10 minutes.

***Activity** How do you keep in contact with the parents/guardians of the children in your class?*

- Are you the kind of teacher that only sends for a parent when there is a problem?

or

- Do you let parents feel that you are willing to talk about the progress and development of their child?

Making parents feel welcome

Make sure that the desks in your classroom are arranged neatly and add interest to the room by displaying a few teaching aids and some examples of pupils' work. You might also like to ask a pupil to arrange three or four chairs in a circle near your desk. As soon as parents arrive, move towards them and show them where to sit. It is more friendly to sit with them rather than behind your desk.

Have all your records ready on your desk so that you can talk to each parent/guardian about the progress, attitude to work and individual problems of their child. They will understand what you are trying to achieve if you can show them their child's exercise books or a piece of work that he/she has done well. As you go over the child's work show his/her parents examples of good and less good work.

Always start and end the interview with something positive. If there is a problem, try to help them by **suggesting ways** that they can help to improve their child's work or attitude to school.

You might find it useful to keep a Parents interview record sheet. Here is a suggested layout.

Date	Points to raise with parents	Points raised by parents	Further Action
Pupil's Name	**Positive points** She is always eager to learn new work.	She enjoys school but they feel that she does not take her work seriously.	**Teacher** (What would parents like you to do?)
Ama	**Problems** Forgets to bring homework to school. Needs help with spelling.		**Parents** (What would you like her parents to do?) Check that she has got her homework before she leaves for school and help her with spelling each evening.

You may want to raise some points yourself. Some of these may have to be discussed in general at a Parent-Teachers Meeting (see Topic 69, Working with the community). There may, however, be issues concerning particular pupils in your class. You will have to be very tactful but if a pupil is not doing well, it may be because of the lack of help or encouragement at home or because the parents do not provide exercise books and writing materials.

At the end of the interview, **go over the actions that you have both agreed to make** once again. Thank the parents for coming and don't forget to arrange to meet them again at the end of the next term.

68 Involving parents in school activities

> ***Activity*** *Involving parents*
>
> Work with other teachers in your school or year group and try to find the names of parents who would be willing to help the school in any way.
>
> - Parents with practical skills that they would share with pupils.
> - Parents willing to help with reading.
> - Parents willing to help with a short field trip.
>
> Would these parents be willing to help regularly, or occasionally?

It is important that parents and guardians are encouraged to take an interest in the activities of the school their children attend. They will then feel proud of its achievements and want to help in its development. Too often schools ask only for donations or expect parents to be involved in fund raising activities. These are important activities and may be necessary, for example, when a new classroom block is needed. There are, however, a number of other ways that parents can be encouraged to give active support to the school.

Helping with class activities

- Listening to reading or helping with project work.
- Helping on school visits or outings.
- Bringing special interests or expertise to the school.

Improving reading levels

Teachers of large classes never have enough time to listen to reading. In a class of 30 pupils, even five minutes for each pupil each week would take more than two hours (see Topic 38, Remedial teaching). Class reading levels would improve if you can find a parent willing to spend an hour once or twice a week listening to pupils read, or willing to tell or read a story to the class at the end of the day.

Special interests

Some parents with special skills such as pottery-making, basket-weaving, sewing or carpentry may be willing to demonstrate or teach these skills during the term.

Visits and field trips

These are always a problem for teachers with large classes. Parents could be asked if they would be willing to accompany a teacher on a school visit.

Can parents still help effectively if they are illiterate?

Illiterate parents often feel, or are made to feel, that they cannot give assistance to the school or their children. Demonstrating skills, helping with field trips or helping to make practical teaching aids are all areas where they could give help that does not depend on the ability to read or write. You will need to make a special effort to show the importance of their support.

Organising help

Some schools are happy to receive assistance from parents. However, if your school has not considered this possibility, it may be necessary to discuss the idea at a Board meeting or the School Management Committee meeting.

If the idea is approved then, as part of an Open Day or during a Parent-Teacher meeting, the head or a senior teacher can tell parents of school plans to use their help in different ways and find out if any parents are willing to volunteer.

You will need very clear guidelines if parental help is to be successful.

- Make it clear to parents when they should come to the school.
- Tell them what help they will be expected to give.
- Explain clearly how they can best give help.

Teachers would then be asked to arrange a meeting with volunteers at the beginning of the term. Together they could plan a programme for the following term. (Some useful guidelines are given below.)

Help with a short field trip

The guidelines should include these details.

- The date, time and location of the visit.
- Which group of children the parent would be looking after.
- Points about the purpose of the visit.
- What the children are going to do (a list of the activities).
- What the parent is expected to do.

Other suggestions for ways that parents can be involved in school activities can be found in Topic 69, Working with the community.

Help with reading

Story-time

A parent willing to read a story would need the following guidelines.

- When they should arrive.
- Where they should sit.
- What story the children are reading and how far they have got in the story.
- Sample questions to maintain pupils' interest and to test how far they understand the story.

Individual reading

Guidelines can be given to parents who help with reading.

Guidelines for parents helping with reading

Total time: 5 minutes per pupil per week.

- Work with each child in a group for five minutes. (This may mean reading aloud with the child or, if they are more confident, listening to each child read on his or her own.)
- Fill in a brief record sheet/check list and make a note of special difficulties.

  Example

  1. *Amina has read up to page 3.*
  2. *She still needs a lot of help even with simple words.*
- Ask the child a few simple questions to see if he/she has understood what he/she is reading. (You will need to provide the questions on a sheet attached to the reading book.)

69 Working with the community

Schools cannot work in isolation. Research now shows that good schools not only provide both effective teaching and learning but also make sure that parents and the community are involved in their development.

In the past, the curriculum taught in schools made very little reference to the local environment and parents, particularly if they were illiterate, felt that they had little to contribute.

Increasingly we have come to recognise that local knowledge and experience has an important contribution to make in the overall education of children. School committees and Parent-Teacher associations are examples of the way in which schools are gradually forming closer relationships with the community. Several sections of this book suggest activities that can be linked to the community. See Topic 69, Working with the community; Topic 68, Involving parents in school activities; Topic 6, Being gender aware and fair; Topic 58, Using the local area.

Teachers can make use of local expertise in many ways

- Sharing knowledge of local resources and skills.
- Involving the community in the development of the school.
- Involving the school in the concerns of the community.

What kind of contribution can a community make?

Parents and other members of the community are often only invited to the school during fund raising activities. When times are hard it can be very difficult to get financial donations. Think of involving the community in the development of the school by asking for a different kind of help. Many might be more willing to give their **knowledge** and **time.**

Linking the community to the school

Teachers are often sent to areas far from their own region. They need to build up local information that will be of use in lessons.

Local history

Invite an elderly man or woman to give a short talk to your pupils describing their life, traditional customs, or what it was like going to school fifty years ago. An elder might also be asked to describe how the community has grown over the past fifty years or to participate in story-telling activities.

Activity *Find out about your school's local area*

Begin a notebook with details of as many things as possible.

- Knowledge of customs and traditions.
- Folk stories, rhymes and legends.
- Traditional farming, animal husbandry and forestry techniques.
- Local plants used for food, medicine or in a local industry.

If you are new to the area, ask your pupils to find out this information from their parents and grandparents as part of a project.

Activity Helping to improve the school facilities and its environment

A school with strong support from the community will have more opportunities for development. This can be done by organising an Open Day or an Improvement Day – a day when parents, teachers, pupils and the community can work together to help in the development of the school.

- They could be involved in the processes of building a new classroom block.
- They could help remove trees that are making classrooms dark.
- They could help to level the compound so that pupils can play safely.
- They could work together to provide safe drinking water and toilets.

Plan to use one of the Improvement Days to develop a school garden.

- Plant flowers, fruit trees or vegetables and label them so that pupils can learn their local and English names.

Many of these ideas cost time and effort rather than money. You will find that it encourages pupils, their parents and the community to take more pride in the achievements of their school.

Working in the community

Among the parents of pupils in your class there will probably be a number of prominent members of the community. Encourage them to talk to your class about their work for about 10–15 minutes and then to answer pupils' questions. You might be able to ask a chief, a lawyer, the local bank manager, a doctor, a farmer, a market trader, a shopkeeper, a vet or a member of the police force to come to school.

Focus on local expertise

Make a list of local industry or crafts such as local building techniques, basket weaving, pottery, fishing, saw-milling, cloth-making and dyeing, carving, oil production, corn-milling or the production of local foods. Invite experts to teach pupils these skills by giving a demonstration of their craft either in the school or in their own work-place if it is near the school. It is important to show your pupils that old skills are still valuable. These presentations not only provide opportunities to develop skills but can also provide background information for writing compositions and give details for projects and careers information.

Raising awareness

Topic 4, The process of learning and Topic 15, Coping with problem behaviour highlight some of the problems such as absenteeism and lack of motivation that prevent pupils from learning. Topic 6, Being gender aware and fair also looks at the importance of treating boys and girls equally. It may be necessary for your school to highlight the importance of education for both boys and girls. Boys are sometimes kept home from school to help with farming or cattle rearing and some communities do not see the value of sending girls to school.

Try to repay community help by working with pupils on a project needed by the community.

70 Using technology in primary teaching

> ***Activity*** *Assessing the sources of information*
>
> Which of the following are available to you?
> Where are they located?
>
> Audio cassettes
> Cameras
>
> Videos
> TV programmes
> Radio programmes
>
> Telephones/fax machines
> Computers/CD ROMs, e-mail and the Internet
> Which of these have you used in your lessons?

This topic looks at the future and the way in which primary school teachers can improve their teaching by using a range of technologies to gain information and ideas from people outside their community.

Using computers

Definitions

ICT: short for Information and Communication Technology.

The Internet: an international network linking millions of computers via telephone lines. It can be used for many different purposes – for teachers it provides a way of getting information and sharing ideas.

e-mail (electronic mail): a means of communication with another person via a computer. Each user has their own address and can send messages to another user at their e-mail address anywhere in the world. Messages are transmitted extremely quickly and are therefore much cheaper to use than a telephone call.

World Wide Web (www): provides a vast amount of information and ideas. Information can be obtained by logging on (connecting) to a Web site that provides information on a particular subject or topic.

At present, very few primary schools in Africa have access to either electricity or telephones so the thought of using the latest computer technology seems very remote. However, many countries are now investing in Teachers' Resource Centres designed to support both primary and secondary schools and their teachers. These centres are usually equipped with typewriters, printers and photocopying machines and many now have computers with access to the Internet. Even though they may be some distance from your school they are well worth visiting. The information you need to make your lesson more interesting can be accessed on the World Wide Web and you can then share this information with your pupils.

Support staff at the centre will be able to help you use the Internet to gain access to education sites. The British Broadcasting Service, for example, can be accessed via **http://www.bbc.co.uk** – http:// tells the computer that a web connection is being made and www shows that it is a World Wide Web address – bbc.co.uk locates the company. Once you gain access to the site you will find information on education programmes. Another site – **www.schoolmaster.net** is interactive and allows teachers to talk to each other about common problems and to share ideas on lessons.

Making use of alternative technologies

ICT may be the future but in the meantime it is possible to make use of a variety of other media to promote learning. Magazines, radio, cassette recorders, television and cameras may be more easily available to you and if they are used imaginatively they can make your lessons more interesting. Some ideas have been given in earlier topics in this book.

Radio and TV and video programmes

Most programmes are not specifically designed as educational programmes but they can provide background information for lessons you might have to teach in the near future, e.g. the pictures and news items of the terrible floods in Mozambique were broadcast on radio and TV across the world. How could you use that information in a lesson?

- An adventure story – 'rescuing a family from the tree tops' or 'the lost child'.
- An environment lesson on the effect of violent tropical storms.
- A discussion on international aid.

Radios and audio cassettes

These allow teachers to make use of the voices of other people and to record material that can be used many times. Batteries are expensive, but there are 'wind-up' radios now on the market that can be tuned in to local and outside broadcasts and some areas are already using solar power. Recording equipment is particularly useful as it can be made interactive, asking questions or setting tasks for pupils to do.

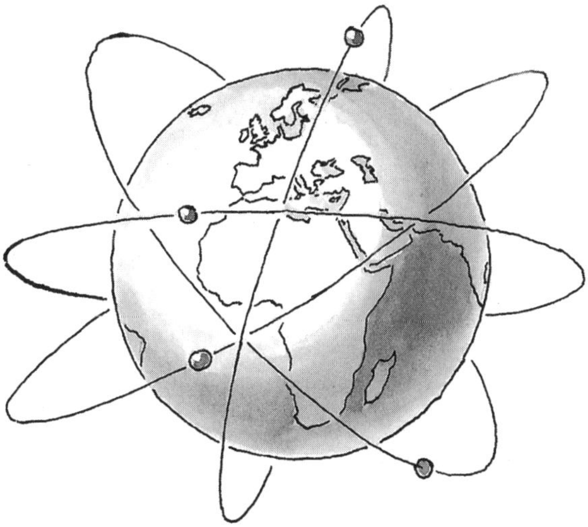

Activity *Using the Internet*

- Exchange lesson notes by e-mail. Write one of your lesson plans in an e-mail and send it to teachers in a TRC in another area asking for comments or ideas.
- Ask for poems or rhymes used by teachers in other areas of the country (e.g. poetry from South Africa can be found on **www.africa.cis.co.za**).
- Ask pupils to write a description of their area for use in a geography lesson. Exchange this information with another school.

Activity *Lesson plans*

- Use your textbook to plan an English lesson making use of an audio cassette as one group activity. You might record a piece for dictation or a series of comprehension questions.
- Borrow a friend's camera and take pictures of your local area. Ask pupils to identify where each photo was taken and then to make a map showing the location of each place.

What other ideas can you link to the subjects you teach in the syllabus?